NATURE

CHANDLER FACSIMILE EDITIONS IN
AMERICAN LITERATURE
Hamlin Hill, *Editor*

ABOUT THIS EDITION

This facsimile edition reproduces a first-state example of the first edition, originally published in September of 1836. For more details, see A Note on the Text.

Science Research Associates, Inc., 259 East Erie Street, Chicago, Illinois 60611

A Subsidiary of IBM

Distributors

NATURE

by

RALPH WALDO EMERSON

A FACSIMILE OF THE FIRST EDITION

With an introduction, a note on the text, and a bibliography prepared by

WARNER BERTHOFF
HARVARD UNIVERSITY

CHANDLER PUBLISHING COMPANY
124 Spear Street, San Francisco, California 94105

LIBRARY OF CONGRESS
CATALOG CARD NO. 68-24232

PRINTED IN
THE UNITED STATES OF AMERICA

CONTENTS

INTRODUCTION

I

"I like my book about nature," Emerson wrote in a much-remarked journal entry, "& wish I knew where & how I ought to live." The sentence is altogether characteristic. We can find in it (learning to look) both the subtle authority of expression in Emerson's best prose—the laconic fitness of thought and phrase which can release yet at the same time almost perfectly conceal some momentous stroke of understanding—and also the tenuity and elusiveness that hang about much of his most familiar work. The entry is dated September 6, 1833. What he calls "my book about nature" existed at that moment only in his head. Short as it finally was, it would not get into print for three more years. The problem of "where & how I ought to live," words casually hitting off the central predicament of his life and vocation, he was never really to solve; characteristically, the act of identifying such a problem in a satisfactory way, defining and isolating it by a transparent brevity of formulation, would somehow absorb the practical energy he would thereafter be willing to devote to it. The inward thought, the original expectation, were sufficient to the end proposed. What further busyness of execution could increase their value to him?

Perhaps every great talent, as it comes forward into its working life, generates some singular and appropriate obstacle to its ideal fulfillment. In any event, may we not see in this affair, at the inception of Emerson's literary life, the quintessential model for the whole of his extraordinarily influential yet somehow disappointing career as an American master? We are reminded how all of Emerson's work may be read as a kind of prolegomenon to some climactic accomplishment which was never quite to be realized—but the full virtue of which in any case could have been traced back to the wholeness and sufficiency of his original conception of it. How then could the work of actually carrying it through seem anything except redundant and pointless? How could it escape that burden of personal embarrassment which, it was Emerson's inclination to feel, our commonest acts and choices in the world are perpetually bringing down on us?

The more obvious reason why this journal entry has attracted notice is that it provides a positive clue to the germination of Emerson's first book. (It also suggests the amiable terms—"I *like* my book . . ."—on which this author preferred to live with his own work, and was perhaps determined to live, during its making; few other writers not swamped in complacency have been so fortunate.) So it is the first half of the sentence that is regularly quoted. The second half, however—so casually and yet, upon examination, so gratuitously added—is what continues to hold attention: "& wish I knew where & how I ought to live." Either it is a *non sequitur,* worth noting in a writer whose more severe critics have sometimes intimated that the *non sequitur* was his chief rhetorical instrument, or it is a singularly revealing stroke of natural wit. The problem of judgment here is typical. Once we begin to get the sense of how Emerson operates as a writer, our experience of reading him is liable to be full of double takes, and our admiration—sluggish and reluctant at first, so little taste remains with us for the mode of pastoral exhortation he seems to employ—springs forward by a geometric progression. It is typical, too, of the problems of Emerson criticism that we may have to risk appearing fancy and sophistical to show off what we guess to be the full import of such deceptively casual remarks. For does not this sentence in its easy, understated way strike to the heart of the specifically modern problem of the writer's occupation? Does it not anticipate that wrenching discovery about the vocation of art that underlies the whole revolution of "modernism" and stands at the center of our literary history since the displacement of classical-humanist norms: the discovery that the writer's, the artist's, life is not a life like any other of good report, needing only to be conducted by the common rules of reason, propriety, good professional discipline, but that it must itself become a new thing, a transfiguring re-creation; that first of all and above all, for the artist himself, *il faut changer la vie?* The work and the life are one. But they are not one in the earlier Romantic sense that the work expresses the life in more or less of its natural totality. Rather, given the conception of a work of a certain order of virtue, the writer is taxed to recreate his whole temporal existence and to begin by considering as seriously as he considers the creative end he has in view precisely *where* and *how* he ought to live in order to undertake that end. *Ought* to live: the auxiliary of obligation is to be noted, surely not being required if the question in Emerson's mind was merely one of satisfactory domestic arrangements.

That Emerson knew himself, at thirty, to be burdened with the problem of vocation, as if his real service of life in the world was just beginning, is itself a fact of prime interest.[1] This burden is one that his first performances as an author inevitably had to labor under. If there is an uncharacteristic awkwardness of address in the book, *Nature*—most commentators agree that there is—one may argue that it has its source here, in a need for self-justification as writer that is not directly relevant to the book's stated theme. Emerson, child of the nineteenth century, was the first of his line to be so afflicted. His father, uncle, grandfathers, and great-grandfathers had been ministers; in all the generations of his ancestry back to the founding of Massachusetts there were men who had shaped their lives to the ministerial calling, though like his father they might regularly suffer pangs of

[1] The general shape this problem took for him and its consequences for his writing are well described in a valuable article by Henry Nash Smith, "Emerson's Problem of Vocation," *New England Quarterly,* XII (1939), 52–67.

doubt whether there was any health in their own pursuit of it; and Emerson himself, properly schooled, had gone to Harvard and, after an interval of schoolteaching and miscellaneous reading, had enrolled in its divinity school in order to become a minister, in fulfillment of the college's chartered function, which was to perpetuate true Christian learning to posterity. In 1826 Emerson was approbated to preach by the Unitarian Association of Middlesex County. By the time he was ordained and established as junior pastor and heir apparent in the pulpit of the influential Second Church in Boston, in 1829, he was already marked out for distinction among the Unitarian churches, which in the early decades of the nineteenth century had assumed the intellectual leadership of the New England province and were guiding its modest revival of learning.

From the first, however, Emerson felt uneasy and constrained as a preacher and in pastoral duties. Yet some singular, barely statable pulpit charm and the gift (already studied and improved) of a direct, simple, natural eloquence won favor with congregations wherever he appeared. Poor health had been his excuse for declining the pastoral offers that came to him as soon as he began preaching.[2] Other causes were operating, as yet inconclusively. He had interrupted his theological studies to take a long winter journey of recovery, in 1826–1827, to South Carolina and Florida; this was shortly after his older brother, William, returned from two years at Gottingen and a disturbing interview with the aged Goethe to announce that in a crisis of conscience he was abandoning the ministry. Emerson's southern journey seems to have served the purpose of reconciling him temporarily to his expected career. It also involved him in a remarkable friendship with Achille Murat, the exiled son of Napoleon's redoubtable marshal and a "noble" and wholly virtuous example of something that up to then, Emerson admitted, he had supposed to be "only a creature of imagination—a consistent Atheist, and a disbeliever in the existence, &, of course, in the immortality of the soul." "My faith in these points," he added, "is strong & I

[2] Professor Jonathan Bishop, tracing out the events of these critical years, has persuasively argued that Emerson's various illnesses "oppressed him most as he prepared and began to practice the duties of the ministry, and left him for good only when he brought himself to abandon it." Such findings increase our sense of how profoundly Emerson's crisis of vocation was acted out. See *Emerson on the Soul* (1964), 166–176.

trust, as I live, indestructible. Meantime I love & honour this intrepid doubter." It seems probable that what as much as anything else induced Emerson to accept the security of the Second Church's offer was his engagement to Ellen Tucker in the winter of 1828–1829; he was married in September, 1829, six months after his ordination. It also seems clear that Ellen's death from tuberculosis early in 1831 (with the prospect of an eventual settlement from her estate) released him to act out entirely according to his inward disposition the continuing crisis of commitment that led him in 1832 to resign his pastorate and abandon the calling to which he had been reared and educated.

Everyone agrees that it was not merely "a change in his opinions concerning the ordinance of the Lord's Supper," as the issue was reported to the Church, that brought this event to pass. Becoming established in the Second Church had only deepened his fundamental restlessness. On January 10, 1832, he wrote: "It is the best part of the man, I sometimes think, that revolts most against his being the minister. His good revolts from official goodness." (On the 21st he urged himself: "Write on personal independence.") Early in June he was more definite: "I have sometimes thought that in order to be a good minister it was necessary to leave the ministry. The profession is antiquated." The Unitarianism he served seemed to him "cold & cheerless," a cerebral faith that existed only by way of its opposition to the old Calvinism and was warmed by very little beyond the barren ardors of controversy. More positively his continued reading in secular literature preoccupied him—Montaigne, Rousseau, Goethe, Schiller, Plato, renaissance drama, modern history and fiction, the British quarterlies (where he first detected Carlyle's strong new voice), and in particular his deeper immersion, after 1829, in Coleridge's *The Friend* and *Aids to Reflection,* in the poems of Wordsworth, and in French and English redactions of the new philosophy of German idealism. He did not want merely to contract into some dreary new cycle of sectarian disputation; if he was interested in converting anybody, it was not on points of doctrine. He did not "think less of the office of a Christian minister"—so at least he wrote his congregation—but he had now another kind of office in mind for himself.

In all Emerson's reading and free meditation an extraordinary new understanding of the inward constitution of the creature, man, began to form.

"There is a capacity of virtue in us, and there is a capacity of vice," he had written in April, 1831, "to make your blood creep." On October 1, 1832, full of the latest *Edinburgh Review* contribution of "my Germanick new-light writer whoever he be," he wrote: "Has the doctrine ever been fairly preached of man's moral nature?" and on the next day: "It is awful to look into the mind of man and see how free we are . . . . Outside, among your fellows, among strangers, you must preserve appearances,—a hundred things you cannot do; but inside,—the terrible freedom!" "Good it is," he added, "to grow familiar with your own thoughts & not shun to speak them." On the 14th: "The great difficulty is that men do not think enough of themselves, do not consider what it is they are sacrificing, when they follow in a herd, or when they cater for their establishment. They know not how divine is a Man." And further:

"Our best friends may be our worst enemies. A man should learn to detect & foster that gleam of light which flashes across his mind from within far more than the lustre of [the] whole firmament without. Yet he dismisses without notice his peculiar thought *because* it is peculiar. The time will come when he will postpone all acquired knowledge to this spontaneous wisdom & will watch for this illumination more than those who watch for the morning . . . . *A man must teach himself* . . . ."

"Projects . . . sprout & bloom in my head," he wrote William Emerson in November, "of action, literature, philosophy." The difficult step of resigning having been taken, at renewed cost to his still fluctuating health, Emerson considered another southern voyage, to the West Indies. This plan quickly gave way to the idea of a European tour, and he sailed for Naples in late December, 1832. In Italy the American pilgrim's familiar shocks of discovery came thick and fast: that legendary Europe was not only hallowed monuments and noble scenes but beggars, pickpockets, filthy laundry blocking your view; that even storied Naples was just another name for the same old world "of man & truth & folly," a name moreover which by its glorious associations made it all the harder "to keep one's judgment upright, & be pleased only after your own way"; that too much gawking at guidebook splendors, even cathedrals, oppressed you with the thought of your own "littleness" as a mere spectator and not a doer, so that to travel grandly is eventually to become self-vexed and self-chagrined; and that—a rising emphasis in his European journal entries—there truly is an American measure and an American difference which the free man of the new world may appeal to for inward assistance. "In Boston," he dryly wrote his Aunt Mary Moody Emerson, from Rome, "they have an eye for improvement, a thing which does not exist in Asia or Africa."

But it was not historical sites and architectural wonders, and certainly not the bothersome company he kept running into of clergymen and earnest seekers debating doctrinal issues, that he chiefly sought out in Europe but poets and men of letters: Landor, Coleridge, Carlyle, Wordsworth. The idea that his true vocation was that of "poet" had taken root in his mind. Seeing these men, he wrote on September 1, 1833, waiting at Liverpool for his ship, "has comforted and confirmed me in my convictions." He had managed not to be disillusioned by his discovery of the ordinariness of their conversation—their petty worldliness, their passing displays of common vanity, their perfect unawareness of this and that important consideration and particularly of "that species of moral truth which I call the first philosophy." All this only increased their usefulness to him; the gap in his own case between circumstance and aspiration seemed less enormous. He felt again the luck of being a man of the new world. America came back to mind as (in a line from the blank-verse "Improvisations" he wrote down when a few days at sea) that land "where man asks questions for which man was made." The "ignorance" (as it seemed to him, on reflection) of even these literary demigods of Europe concerning true religion; their confusing it with worldly institutions and observances; the degree to which their complicity with the given world of accredited thoughts made them reluctant to say plainly at every moment that "the purpose of life seems to be to acquaint a man with himself"; their inability to act consistently as men and writers on the revelation "that God is in every man"—these things sent him home in a double exaltation. He had seen natural human greatness, superior always to its customary manifestations, and he had freely imagined something even loftier and finer.

Yet Emerson, at thirty, was also aware that he had been challenged to meet his English worthies on their own ground. He took to heart Carlyle's warning that mere dissidence, mere rebellion, would not be enough—and that this might indeed be the only substance, so far, of the celebrated "American principle." It was because his new vocation was built upon a new life-faith, because it was, finally, religious, that Emerson's deeply conservative and deferential mind could embrace it so confidently. But what precisely was this faith and how was it to be articulated? The ripened and settled modes of understanding displayed in the forms of European literature, as in all the phenomena of European civilization, could not simply be disregarded. Hearing of some new message, "the men of Europe will say, Expound; let us hear what it is that is to convince the faithful and at the same time the philosopher," and they would, Emerson felt, be right. To find a way of satisfying this double audience—of incontrovertibly expounding as well as exhorting and advocating; speaking to the intellect as well as to feeling; yet expounding in such a way as not to lose the living pulse and nerve of the spirit's activity—was the literary task now before him. It was success in this task which would justify his new vocation—and which, in the achieving, would set him apart from the rhapsodic antinomianism of dissidence and self-assertion that was beginning to blaze up afresh in the New England province.

II

In the years following Emerson's return from Europe the pattern of his outward career as an author was secured and with it a material solution to the problem of "where and how to live." During the winter of 1833–1834 he lectured, chiefly in Boston, on the uses of the study of nature and on his Italian travels, and he continued through the next two winters with lecture series on the lives of great men—he selected artists (Michelangelo, Milton) and spiritual heroes (Luther, George Fox, Burke)—and on the history of English literature. Thereafter the spoken lecture was both his chief source of earned income and the prose form he mainly used for his published writings. He moved from Boston to his grandfather Ripley's house in Concord in the fall of 1834; a year later he married again and, with his wife's income added to the Tucker legacy, settled into a house of his own in Concord.

Emerson's lectures, journals, and letters for 1833–1836 are crammed with formulations of his developing thought, that "main thought" which his writing, as John Jay Chapman said, "is never far from." For November, 1833, we find this journal entry: "Nature is a language & every new fact that we learn is a new word . . . ." In March of the next year: "The subject that needs most to be presented, developed, is the principle of Self reliance, what it is, what it is not, what it requires, how it teaches us to regard our friends." In September: "Perhaps you cannot carry too far the doctrine of self-respect." Bold undertakings are sketched that now and then anticipate literary innovations of a later time. Thus on November 19, 1833: "Wrote to Charles yesterday of the amount of meaning in life: *dum tacet clamat* . . . . If a susceptible man should lay bare his heart"—this, fifteen years before the entry in Poe's *Marginalia* that electrified Baudelaire and produced the purgative journal, "Mon coeur mis à nu." (Emerson himself would undertake this exorbitant task perhaps only in the confessional essay, "Experience," and even there would choose to examine the data of his own life altogether impersonally.) In all that he writes during these years a double truth is regularly postulated. (1) The human individual stands at the center of the experienced universe and can find within himself the resources for whatever he is called to in life. (2) The surrounding universe—

nature—supports him totally and continuously and speaks to him at every moment. The relation is dynamic: the universe of being may be trusted to communicate actively out of whatever force it is animated by to whatever of animate force resides in man, and thus *will* call him forth into his correspondent being.

We see, looking back into earlier journals and sermons, that something like this double truth has been with Emerson from the first, though his early expression of it was more conventional. Originally his stress was on how the "kindling excitement" man feels within himself, the power to transcend the common "weakness of humanity," comes from man's discovery that he may "lean on omnipotence" (May, 1828), or it was on how a "voice" speaks within man and satisfies his yearning for "a faith satisfactory to his own proper nature," telling him that "God is within him, that *there* is the celestial host."[3] In this earlier form, of course, both thought and expression were still coming directly out of long-standing Puritan tradition,

[3] *Young Emerson Speaks,* ed. A. C. McGiffert (1938), 200.

whose most creative participants—reconstituters of the central faith like Jonathan Edwards, adherents to new sectarian rites like the Quakers, Baptists, and Swedenborgians—had regularly moved toward some version of the thought announced in Emerson's first sermon, in 1826, that God "is not so much the observer of your actions, as he is the potent principle by which they are bound together." The New England theology had long since turned inward, psychologizing its essential witness, where it had not dried up altogether. And as much as any observable distinction of statement, it was the familiarity of Emerson's thought, its rootedness in regional and sectarian tradition, that touched the audience he was addressing, giving him in turn the confidence to speak his mind ever more bluntly and freely. He knew this himself (tallying his "advantages," he once set them down as simply "the total New England"), and his best critics have always recognized it. So Charles Ives—in whom the original energy of Emerson's thought survived perhaps the longest without dilution, being renewed in his own work as composer—shrewdly observed that the Emersonian "philosophy or . . . religion (or whatever you will call it)" was not simply an intellectual construction but a source of spiritual energy that acquired, for its adherents in covenant-minded communities like Concord, "some of the functions of the Puritan church."

The literary overform Emerson was using was the sermon; his lectures and, later, essays have the appearance of lay sermons. The old Puritan sermon was intended like any other to inspire the activity of faith and provided a regular place for spirit-lifting perorations. But in Calvinist New England, bred to the expectation of a reasoned faith and a learned ministry able to expound it, care was taken to ground this effort of inspiration and encouragement in rational demonstration, to support it with the other comforts of philosophic or doctrinal authority and sufficient argumentative proof. By the early nineteenth century, however, the old proofs from Scripture and the general framework of scholastic argumentation (no longer in itself considered to be divinely appointed, as it had been by the first Puritans) were not enough to persuade reasoning minds. Between the founding of Massachusetts and the 1830's a long revolution had taken place, intellectual as well as political and social. On the one hand new, empirically authorized, "scientific" descriptions of nature and of human understanding had gained acceptance and had become increasingly elaborate (but also increasingly truistic) in the philosophically busy century after Newton and Locke. On the other hand, more recently, a sophisticated secular understanding of the historical origins of Christian worship had emerged, with the beginnings of the so-called higher criticism. Now to the freest minds of the new age these new doctrines were not simply a troublesome challenge to the old beliefs. They were fascinating and absorbing in themselves. And Emerson was one of those post-Enlightenment minds who saw that, far from overthrowing faith, these doctrines might provide a powerful new endorsement of it—*if* rightly understood, rightly interpreted. Thus his broad interest in natural science, on which he lectured in 1833–1834 and to which he returned at the start of his series on "The Philosophy of History" in the winter of 1836–1837. In holding to the general structure of the sermon, so firmly established in New England as an instrument of reasoned inquiry as well as of declamatory faith, he was holding to a method of discourse which was reassuringly familiar to his audience, yet within which he could present his new understanding in, broadly speaking, philosophical as well as inspirational form.

The lectures he offered between 1833 and 1836 are literate and emphatic, and by every outward sign they were successful. Each season Emerson was more widely in demand in eastern Massachusetts—he was also supply-preaching on invitation—and his platform reputation spread rapidly (culminating in the moderately precocious honor of invitations to deliver the Phi Beta Kappa address at Harvard in 1837 and the address to the graduating class at the Divinity School in 1838). But Jonathan Bishop is surely right in suggesting that these early lectures "fell somewhat short of fulfilling the fine promise he made to himself on his return from Europe to say nothing that did not wholly match his own purposes." In part this was probably because the subjects he lectured on were determined more than would later be the case by other people's interest and expectation (tell us about Italy, tell us about English literature). In any case these lectures, in print, seem rather too monotonously assertive. The arguments they advance lack natural flow; they do not yet do what Chapman said the mature Emerson always does at his best, which is to keep close, like the truest poetry, to the psychology of real life and real experience.

The fact is that the very conditions which gave the rapid opening out of Emerson's career in letters so natural and, as it seems, inevitable a configuration—first, that his thought by the fullness of his personal commitment to it had become second nature with him and was everywhere revealed; second, that the form of the sermon or inspirational treatise lay so conveniently to hand—were also, in subtle ways, obstacles to achieving a decisive eloquence. His tendency, never entirely overcome, was to say everything at once; to put his whole message into one masterful assertion, one comprehensive and immediately persuasive formula. Everyone recognizes this in Emerson. He is perhaps the nearest thing we have in Anglo-American literature to an introspective maxim-writer; he applies the New England predilection for the folk proverb (the form that Franklin, who represents another strain in Emerson's province inheritance, mastered first) to the subject matter of the great French moralists; and one notices that his European admirers—like Proust, who took several epigraphs from Emerson for *Plaisirs et Jours*—have accepted him as a master in this vein and have not thought to put him down, as Henry James did, as

Thus through Nature is there a striving ~~for~~ upward. Commodity points to a greater good. Beauty is nought until the spiritual element. Language refers to that which is to be said."

Here at last are the classifications that open the way. "Nature," "Commodity," "Beauty" (with a subsection on its "spiritual element"), and "Language" become the successive chapters which fill out the first half of *Nature* as we have it; supplemented by "Discipline," a more general classification that, it is specified, "includes" the preceding ones, these classifications in fact compose the book's whole rising argument.

Professor Ralph L. Rusk, in the standard modern biography of Emerson, says simply that "chapters of *Nature* . . . were growing toward completion in his journals" all through the 1833–1836 period, but the journal evidence does not support this description of the book's emergence.[7] The evi-

[7] *The Life of Ralph Waldo Emerson* (1949), 203. Further on (p. 240) the less positive and rather more accurate statement is made that *Nature* "had grown slowly out of his journals, letters, sermons, and lectures."

In a letter of June 28, 1836, Emerson wrote that his "little book is nearly done" but also that his plan was "to follow it . . . with another essay, 'Spirit'; and the two shall make a decent volume." It would appear that the

dence is worth setting out in detail, at the risk of getting bogged down in textual minutiae. (Readers are referred, in this chapter-by-chapter examination, to the facsimile text which follows.)

1. Of the "Introduction," elements of three or four sentences—no more—occur in rough form in journal entries of January and June, 1836 (*Journals and Miscellaneous Notebooks,* V, 117, 174: I follow here the correlations made by the journals' most recent editors). What is most interesting, however, is that we find nothing in the journals of the introduction's crucial "philosophic" definition of "nature."

2. It is "Chapter I" (untitled in the printed text but called "Nature" in the table of contents) that makes the fullest use of journal material. This chapter's exalted opening paragraph was roughed out in entries of March, 1834 (*JMN,* IV, 266–

---

complete structure was not worked out until the last minute. On August 8 Emerson wrote his brother William that there was still "one crack in it not easy to be soldered or welded"—most probably this is the "crack" between "Discipline" and the important opening paragraphs of "Idealism," where the argument turns off sharply in a new direction. He added that he hoped to finish within the week. On August 27, according to his journal, he received the first proof-sheet.

267), and July, 1835 (*JMN,* V, 73), the latter entry giving the last two sentences of the paragraph in very nearly their final form. The second halves of the next two paragraphs make use of passages from April, 1835 (*JMN,* V, 29–30), and January, 1836 (*JMN,* V, 113); the second of these is much recast. The next-to-last paragraph in this chapter derives from an entry of late June, 1836 (*JMN,* V, 179)—when the book was being rushed to completion.

But the most interesting case in Chapter I is the fourth paragraph, containing the great sustained dithyramb on man's experience in physical nature. The basic notation of a "wild delight" and of the incessant correspondence of hour and mood was set down on December 8, 1834 (*JMN,* IV, 355). An entry for March 17, 1835 (*JMN,* V, 17), gives us a draft of the sentence beginning, "Nature is a setting." The key sentences beginning, "In the presence of nature," and, "Almost I fear," trace to a single entry for March 26 (*JMN,* V, 24–25).[8] The two sentences beginning with the second use of the three times repeated phrase, "In the woods," are distilled from an entry of February 8, 1836

[8] The second of these sentences underwent an important change in the 1849 edition: see below, lxv–lxvi.

(*JMN,* V, 119). But the last "In the woods" sentence, immediately following, appears to have no particular source in the journals; we also notice that it is the most abstract and philosophical of the three. The climax the paragraph now rises to was worked out in its main sequence and in many verbal details on March 19, 1835 (*JMN,* V, 19), and thus existed from the first in near relation to several of the sentences leading up to it. On the other hand its most extraordinary flourishes are not to be found in the original entry: neither the breathtaking phrase about the vanishing of "all *mean* egotism" (which seems to me one of the irreducible formulations of a distinction central to the whole of romantic and modern literature) nor the startling "transparent eye-ball" figure. To this whole passage and these additions, not universally admired, we must return, for they are of critical importance to Emerson's literary success in *Nature*.

3. Apart from Chapter I, what the evidence seems to show is that not much of the text of *Nature* and almost nothing of its compositional design antedate the spring and summer of 1836. In the short chapter, "Commodity," a figure of speech and two separate sentences trace to entries of March, 1836 (*JMN,* V, 145–146). More of "Beauty" preexists.

The ecstatic passage asking for the supreme gifts of "health and a day" dates to January, 1835 (*JMN,* V, 13: but the journal entry lacks the witty turn at the end connecting the two great contending epistemological schools, English and German, to different hours of the day's experience), and entries for October and November of 1835 (*JMN,* V, 96–97, 108) support the middle part of the chapter. The three-section structure of "Beauty," however, was not conceived until an entry of May 31, 1836 (*JMN,* V, 166). Less of "Language" was written out in the journals, though this chapter does contain the earliest recorded sentence of the final text, the quotation from Swedenborg in the first paragraph of subsection "3" which Emerson found in the *New Jerusalem Magazine* for July, 1832 (*JMN,* IV, 33). One other early journal entry, from 1833 (*JMN,* IV, 216), has special interest because it sets out as a question—"Why can we find a spiritual meaning in every natural fact?"—the gist of the three remarkable propositions that "Language" opens with. "Discipline": the scattered journal passages transposed into this chapter all come, except for one quotation, from 1836 (February, March, June: *JMN,* V, 124–125, 134–137, 174–177). "Idealism": the larger part of subsection "1" derives from two 1834 entries (*JMN,* IV, 277, 323). Otherwise the chapter makes use, mostly towards the end, of a scattering of entries from these same months in 1836. "Spirit": part of the last paragraph traces to August, 1835 (*JMN,* V, 82); of the few other traceable sentences all but one are from June, 1836 (*JMN,* V, 171, 182–84). *4.* The most extensive journal borrowings, after Chapter I, appear in the last chapter, "Prospects," and the odd thing about these is that most of them go into the two passages attributed to the "Orphic poet," deriving from a single sequence of entries for June 22, or June 22–23, 1836 (*JMN,* V, 179–183).[9] There are several effective additions to this

[9] What this tells us about the much-debated identity of the "Orphic poet," to whom important closing affirmations in *Nature* are given, is not clear. The journal entries accompany the notation of a memorable visit by Bronson Alcott, who "made here some majestic utterances"—"but so inspired me," Emerson obscurely adds, "that even I forgot the words often." Kenneth Walter Cameron (*Emerson the Essayist,* 1945) has argued that the Orphic poet is Emerson himself and that Alcott only provided general inspiration. Professor Rusk, on the other hand, reviewing Cameron's argument (*American Literature,* XVII, 272–274), was clearly right in pointing out that the two leading facts in evidence—that no such passages appear in Alcott's own work of the same moment, *Psyche,* and that Emerson did not put what he wrote down inside quotation

material in the final printed version, in the form of supplementary and transitional phrases—and one such is perhaps the best remembered sentence in the whole of *Nature,* being the summary message that readers were to take back into their active lives: "Build therefore your own world."

III

Nature, then, is synthetic in construction and far from seamless. From the traditional sermon it borrows the scheme of a predicative series of topics and subtopics leading to an inspiring peroration (and so permits itself a certain mixture of styles or voices); from contemporary learning the device of an original structure of classifications.[10] Emerson himself showed no great satisfaction with the result.

---

marks—are not clear proofs of Emerson's sole authorship.

It seems unarguable that Alcott's visit and his conversation, in late June of 1836, exerted some kind of influence on the book's peroration. At the least they may have given Emerson the idea of attributing much of it, by familiar convention, to another voice expressing a purer inspiration.

[10] F. O. Matthiessen (*American Renaissance,* 67–68) suggests another model, the prose Meditation. Professor Louis Martz has called attention to the widespread use of this model in seventeenth-century poetry, for which Emerson and his New England contemporaries had not lost their provincial taste.

Once the book was out, he hardly spoke of it. He wrote to Carlyle in September of 1836: "This is only a naming of topics on which I would gladly speak and gladlier hear"—a description that fixes on the compositional element, the sequence of chapters and chapter headings discussed above, which Emerson cared for least. He never used this scheme again for meditative discourse. The topical divisions are not arbitrary; the arrangement they fall into is rational and progressive; but Emerson is not very interested in them and certainly does not feel bound to them. They are the scaffolding on which the fabric of vivid instances and affirmations is hung out—and hung out, except for a few key passages, quite casually. As in the essays, the local clusters and runs of eloquence and fervor, along with various maxims, are what we mostly remember from *Nature,* not the march of its argument.

Yet we can be misled if we conclude too hastily that Emerson was only making a show of logical system in *Nature,* in deference to common expectation. The fact is that he worked forward according to two seemingly contradictory standards of truth. The old Calvinist suspicion of unmediated spiritual enthusiasm still carried weight with him. It might be true, as he affirmed in the "Introduction" (with a modern artist's natural pragmatism), that man "acts [the meaning he seeks] as life, before he apprehends it as truth," since man is wise not in the skillful exercise of his reasoning faculty but in the degree to which the whole incessant process of ordinary life has made supple and precise "the Hand of the mind" (the fine phrase used in "Discipline"). It might also be true, by the paradox Emerson would announce at Harvard a year later, that "books are for the scholar's idle times," and that Man Thinking has more important work to do than practice argumentation. Yet it remained axiomatic with him that every natural divination of truth *would* reveal itself, under scrutiny, to be rational and logically intelligible; and as we noted earlier, he continued to believe that it was a main part of the writer's responsibility to demonstrate this and thus to convince "the philosopher" as well as "the faithful."

But as it had become the very substance of Emerson's thought that truths of intellect were always truths of natural experience, so it seemed to him that the most important function of the writer was not to pronounce the truths but to activate the experience.[11] The result can be described in either of two ways. It is essentially philosophic discourse of which, however, a main rhetorical purpose is to conceal its own reliance on philosophic argument, fostering the illusion that what is said is wholly self-evident and naturalistic. Or it is essentially prophecy and exhortation (revelation of what is; encouragement towards what therefore must be done) that gains its decisive authority not only by surreptitiously appropriating concepts of systematic philosophy (in the manner of much of Wordsworth's psychological poetry) but by submitting these concepts to further critical refinement. Following this view, we see how Chapman's assertion that Emerson "bears no relation whatever to the history of philosophy" will have to be radically qualified, though we see what Chapman was responding to. John Dewey understood Emerson's tactics better (and the continuity between Emerson's thought and that of the major pragmatists

[11] This conception of effective discourse renews in secular terms the logic of the old evangelical sermon, and not just as vulgarly practiced. It had been Jonathan Edwards's concern as well as the Wesleyans' to make his hearers *live* the doctrinal truth he was preaching, through the sensible fullness and harmony of his rehearsal of it.

is central to American intellectual history): "he takes the distinctions and classifications which to most philosophers are true in and of and because of their systems, and makes them true of life, of the common experience of the everyday man." Emerson's prophetic criticism of life and human capacity is the more compelling because it is adjusted to philosophic premises as well as to experience and feeling, and it is the more complete because it includes a radical critique of these premises.

Here Emerson's wit and irony play their part. They are conceptual as well as verbal. The more one recognizes how Emerson was at once forcing explosive philosophic issues upon the argument of *Nature* and yet keeping them at bay, the more one sees that even Chapman's tribute to the book's "extraordinary beauty of language" is less than adequate to its special distinction. A transcendental or idealist theory of phenomenal reality is obviously at hand as Emerson proceeds, and is the asset he seeks to convert to effective use.[12] But he understands that natural experience (rhetorically his

[12] Its sources—Platonic, Swedenborgian, Berkeleyan, German—have been widely discussed and need not concern us here.

final court of appeal) both endorses and subverts this theory, and that the skeptical argument against it has as much force to the sensitive intelligence as the evidences, mostly psychological and moral, in its favor. The argument he must disarm is thus an argument in his own mind and experience—his own and, he is sure, everyone's, as sentient and reflective beings. In the book, *Nature,* it becomes that argument with himself from which, as Yeats said, the true poet will make something beyond mere rhetoric. Emerson further sees that it is a wholly natural argument, that it is constitutional to the mind of man—by day, so to speak, experience is indeed material and sensual but by night it can turn fantastic and visionary—and so he is not disabled by it but sets about making it a positive resource.

That is to say, he writes dialectically, in the root sense. His sentences, as they advance, actively converse with one another. As Josephine Miles has said (*Style and Proportion,* 70), the usual connectives are omitted, but the connection is there. It is this continuous dialectical factor that overcomes the alleged discontinuity of Emerson's rhetoric—as it also helps to overcome the dispersion that naturally accompanies (as, say, in Alcott's writing) the effort to express purely a vision of experience as a universal hieroglyph: when everything is equally and endlessly significant, how does one ever decide which particular significance to bring forward next? Dialectical, even tautological, however, rather than syllogistic (Professor Miles's word): Emerson's writing proceeds from a way of talking with himself rather than from a reasoned scheme for completing arguments. Every really penetrating account we have of Emerson—invariably some essential division or doubleness of temperament is stressed—suggests that this way of talking was singularly personal. It is regularly seen, moreover, as the source of his peculiar combination of effectiveness (of voice) and insubstantiality (of demonstration). Chapman called him "the only writer we have had who has wholly subdued his vehicle to his temperament"—an ambiguous tribute, surely—while Ives remarks that "so close a relation exists between his content and expression, his substance and manner, that if he were more definite in the latter he would lose power in the former." For good or bad this is the way Emerson exists as a writer, and it is fundamentally, we see, the way of an artist. So William James understood the matter:

". . . the man Emerson's mission culminated in his style, and if we must define him in one word, we have to call him Artist. He was an artist whose medium was verbal and who wrought in spiritual materials."

—a judgment (applying, after all, to many poets and even narrative writers) which Charles Feidelson has perceptively amplified:

"He was an artist in the medium of theory—in short, a dialectician—and his doctrines are better regarded as themes of his discourse than as elements of a system."

1. Perhaps the best example in *Nature* of Emerson's dialectical art is also the most important passage philosophically; it is the opening of Chapter VI, "Idealism." Up to this point Emerson has been filling out the headings given in the breakthrough journal entry of 27 March, 1836 (see p. xxxiii). Starting from a rhapsodic assertion in Chapter I of the impact of what we commonly call "nature" upon our perceptions and feelings, he has enumerated in a rising succession nature's practical "uses." As "commodity" it supplies us materially; as "beauty" it satisfies the spirit's higher wants and needs; as the demonstrable source of "language," and a language itself, it both creates meaning and provides the means of expressing, communicating, remembering meanings, and is thus the specific instrument of our "knowledge" and "power"; in all of these ways it is a constant "discipline," educating us towards fulfillment of our innate capacity for being. All aspects of Emerson's studied gift of eloquence—his phrase-making, his witty mixture of pulpit hyperbole and satirical colloquialism ("whilst we use this grand cipher to expedite the affairs of our pot and kettle"), his active delight in putting words to the inexhaustible variety and yet fitness of things—contribute to making these successive assertions telling.

They contribute to something else, however: to keeping in abeyance those "philosophical considerations" which he himself intruded—not very relevantly, it may have seemed at the time—in the last paragraph of his short introduction. Here "nature" was defined in a different way, not as *what is,* which variously speaks to us, but as *what we are not* ("all that is separate from us . . . which Philosophy distinguishes as the NOT ME"). It is object, we are subject—the definition is Kantian and Coleridgean—and as it includes not only the nonhuman physical universe but also the products of past human action ("art, all other men and my own body"), we see that Emerson's definition is epistemological: "nature" is the name we give to what we find or might find, at each new moment, in our consciousness's continuous apprehension of things.

But how do we know where all this "really" comes from, or whether it is "really" there; whether our knowledge of it is true knowledge; whether its meaning to us has any objective validity? This is the particular philosophical question that Emerson, breaking with the comfortable academic philosophy of common-sense realism which Harvard instruction and the Unitarian faith were based on, knew had to be faced. Since Berkeley and Hume the skeptical argument—that the names we give to what is objective to us have no foundation except in our act of naming, and that the speech of nature to our minds cannot be proved to be anything but subjective illusion—could not be ignored, particularly if a doctrine of "man's moral nature" and his duty to "teach himself" was at stake.

So in Chapter VI Emerson turned back upon his own demonstration to raise this awkward question—or rather, in the phrasing he uses (a doubt "perpetually suggests itself"), to indicate right away that the importunities of skepticism are intrinsic to experience. Such doubt always exists (thus the adverb) and it rises spontaneously (thus the reflexive). It is also a "noble" doubt: the higher part of our minds receives it. We see at once that Emerson is going to color and dramatize this risky step in his argument (self-imposed, but unavoidable) as richly as any other. Every phrase will count: every rift (to borrow Keats's famous charge to Shelley, not irrelevant here) is to be loaded with ore. The process has already begun in the more-than-transitional first paragraph of "Idealism," a striking example of rhetoric that is both idealizing and dangerously exact. "Thus is the unspeakable but intelligible and practicable meaning of the world conveyed to man the immortal pupil . . . ." "Unspeakable": this despite all in the way of articulated meaning that an introduction and five preceding chapters have eloquently advanced. With the general argument explicitly joined on the plane of "language," the case for believing that nature can have effective "meaning" for us can hardly have taken a bleaker turn. But at the same time, "intelligible" and "practicable": this meaning cannot be spoken in so many words, cannot be captured in measured discourse, yet it can be grasped by the mind ("the Hand of the mind") and it can be acted on. This will be so insofar as man continues to be what he essentially is, "the immortal pupil," a being whose unique capacity for *education* is the one thing that can lead him out of the death cell of meaninglessness, of which the chief experienced symbols are the irreversible succession of time and the intrinsic separateness ("philosophically considered") of consciousness.

Emerson's tactics quickly become clear. He has raised, or turned to face, a shattering philosophic objection to everything he has been saying—the audible heightening of his language is the immediate sign of this argumentative crisis—but he is not necessarily going to answer it in the philosophic language usually employed. This "noble doubt," he means to suggest, represents a natural turn of mind and way of speaking, and it leads to certain further ways of speaking. That these have often been resigned or despairing in tone is not his affair. It is by his own developed way of speaking—on both sides of the issue at once and with the full resources of his rhetoric—that he will deal with it. He will deal with it melodramatically, histrionically; there will be a resounding verbal enactment of dealing with it, designed to produce an impression that it has been dealt with. (That trickery and subterfuge are naturally in the air is suggested at once; I suspect that Emerson wanted the full range of connotation in the verb, "conspire," which ends the opening paragraph.)

So he proceeds, subordinating one argumentative step after another to a manner of speaking that ironically exaggerates and even contradicts, but also getting the fullest supporting charge from the common words accompanying. "It is a sufficient account [not "true" or "complete"—we don't know that—just "sufficient"] of that Appearance we call the World [what could be more frankly skeptical?] that God will teach a human mind . . ." ["*will* teach": if the sentence cadence is to come out right, can one avoid giving the auxiliary a positive emphasis?]. So far this sentence claims a lot, and all too simply—and Emerson now undercuts the substance of it by admitting flat out that all the instructed mind really gets in this divine schoolroom is "a certain number of sensations," to which, finding some to be "congruent" with others, it casually applies certain very simple names.

But in the circumstances what more can the mind do? Let us admit it: our impotence to tell whether these sensations and names are objectively valid is an "utter impotence." Yet such sensations do come to us, and have such intensity that the names we have arbitrarily given them are themselves strangely exciting to recall. And that being so, "what difference does it make"—what difference *to us*—whether these sensations "correspond with outlying objects" that exist apart from our apprehension? If Orion is not really there in the heavens (the choice of that conspicuous non-entity, a constellation, with its poetical name, serves Emerson's purpose here in an obvious way), then it is there in "the soul," which must itself be nothing less than a "firmament" if it can contain so magnificent an "image." That image, moreover, has such gorgeousness that we find it the most natural thing in the world to say that some creative power we are moved to call a "god" must have put it there. However we explain or fail to explain the matter, "the relations of parts" (the way *we* see it) "and the end of the whole" (the way *we* use it) remain the same for us. Whatever such a thing may be in itself, it's all one to us.

Emerson is in fact being solidly philosophical here, as precise about the mind's relation to the phenomenal world as anybody had learned to be by 1836. The philosophic supports he does *not* fall back on are noteworthy. He does not appeal to concepts of innate ideas or of metaphysical or ontological necessity, and his passing reference to "God" as the presumed source of our instruction is doubly undercut: by the unexalted phrase about "a certain number of sensations," as noted above, and by the almost derisive parody-echo of his second, lower-case appeal to divinity, "some god paints the image." The constitutive idea here is rather Kant's unity of apperception, the principle that what comes into our minds (whatever its source, and also whatever its effect on us: the impressions that create skepticism as well as those that create faith) must come in the same way, since it is received by the same organ, the same mysteriously separate and single instrument. More than that cannot be said, except willfully. In the crisis of his argument Emerson maintains Kant's own reserve about knowledge of ultimate reality, being for the moment more discreet than many neo-Kantians. But he also knows the vivid splendor of our sensible perceptions and the consoling magnificence of our names and observations, and he thus counterpoints his second "What is the difference?" with a full-voiced evocation of the wonders we do perceive, land and sea, innumerable celestial bodies, "deep yawning under deep, and galaxy balancing galaxy." These may indeed be only "appearances," but if appearances so extraordinary do exist, how can man's natural "faith" in them—if that is what he is moved to—be anything less than "constant"? And even if they exist only in that appearance-registering mechanism, the mind, or even if (to return to the image opening Chapter I) some of them should appear there only once in a thousand years, then the occasion surely requires no less a word than "apocalypse"—"the apocalypse of the mind"—and here, too, I think Emerson wanted both the proper meaning of revelation or uncovering and the vulgar meaning of some abrupt, utmost convulsion of natural existence.

Again we note that it is not to Emerson's purpose to specify his philosophic authority—and there is, for scholarship, a question how much of Kant he knew beyond English and French redactions and the gossip of the learned quarterlies. There is a question, too, whether naming Kant or any other "new" philosopher wouldn't have stirred up inconvenient prejudices in his audience, besides jeopardizing the whole scheme of arguing from "nature." Emerson does, however, somewhat uncharacteristically, make explicit the philosophic debate he is concerned here to recreate as natural to experience. He speaks directly of "the Ideal theory" and the common charge (attributed promptly to "the frivolous") that it affects "the stability of nature." And precisely at this point the intricate verbal dialectic we have been tracing stalls for a moment. The ironic back-and-forth of subject and predicate, substantive and modifier, gives way to naked assertion. "God" reappears, and what He will and will not do is set down as beyond argument—though the sentence as a whole is more charming than intimidating: "God never jests with us" and can be relied on to keep the "procession" of nature in step. (The special tone here is one that Emily Dickinson also mastered.) The next sentence opens down to the foundations of Emerson's purposes as a writer. It brings forward the main object of the whole book, which is to call man forth out of the sickroom of inaction into the kingdom of his own created being. The substance of it is not metaphysical but psychological. The verb dominates: "Any distrust of the permanence of laws, would paralyze the faculties of man."[13] This

[13] So in the Divinity School "Address": "O my friends, there are resources in us on which we have not drawn." And in "The Transcendentalist": "We are miserable with inaction."

"permanence" of nature may be only a hypothesis, but it is that one hypothesis that is constitutional to man, that his "wheels and springs are all set to."

Having put the real issue—active being or paralysis, life or non-life—on the line, Emerson returns now to his usual mode of aphorism and figure-making, though not before admitting once again that "the question of the absolute existence of nature still remains open" and that nothing further can be said except that the particular impressions that do come to us do not in themselves "shake our faith." The rest of the book describes the natural behavior of that action of being which is creaturely faith. When towards the end of Chapter VI the question of "the reality of the external world" is resumed, Emerson argues simply from decorum: "But I own there is something ungrateful in expanding too curiously the particulars of the general proposition that. . . ." At the last, admitting that "the ideal theory" is "that view which is most desirable to the mind," he flaunts this subjectivity as one of the theory's chief advantages, for the desire in question is, again, not gratuitous but constitutional; it is the mind's and the heart's, proper response ("philosophy and virtue" together) to the compelling miracle of appearances.

2. The "self-concentration" of Emerson's style (to borrow again from Keats's description of the "modern" artist's character) seems to exist in close relation to an essential distrust of affirmative argument. Emerson shared, as did Thoreau, the Romantic suspicion that silence might be more truthful to the nature of things than speech, though both writers were kept from carrying this thought to Carlylean or Symbolist extremes by their inherited loyalty (like Kierkegaard's) to the practice of edifying discourse.[14] The idea of the purity of meaning in silence was a constant spur to writing better —or to not writing at all. A sentence from one of Landor's "imaginary conversations" stuck in Emerson's mind: "no man ever argued so fairly as he might have done." His invincibly high-minded Concord friends hardly encouraged his trying. A journal entry for August 2, 1835, reports that his

[14] The writing of Kierkegaard, among their European contemporaries, seems especially relevant to that of the Concord transcendentalists. Perhaps not sweetness of temperament so much as the materially freer equilibrium of Concord life in the 1830's—surely the freest established society the world has ever known; hence its writers' preoccupation with the subjective uses of freedom—withheld Emerson and Thoreau from Kierkegaard's more savagely ironic and subversive exercises in this traditional mode.

gifted brother Charles had thrown doubt on the whole business of keeping a journal, and he could only reply, "I must scribble on," though the sentences end "in babble." Recording a long conversation with Thoreau in November, 1838, Emerson reports himself "acceding" to Thoreau's assertion that the act of writing usually betrays the thought and prevents the writer from doing justice to the full human experience from which his thought proceeded; here, Emerson added, was "the tragedy" of all art, "that the artist was at the expense of the man . . . ." The Concord atmosphere in the early days of the transcendentalist movement was oppressive with this kind of deterrent perfectionism. The very effort to overcome it confirmed it. "Speech is the sign of partiality, difference, ignorance," Emerson had written a month earlier, "and the more perfect the understanding between men, the less need of words." So, too, with man's understanding of nature. What does the "wise man" eventually see but that every fact contains all truths? The practical result is that the more we try to speak some particular truth, the more our words fail us:

". . . as we advance, every proposition, every action, every feeling, runs out into the infinite. If we go to affirm anything, we are checked in our speech by the need of recognizing all other things, until speech presently becomes rambling, general, indefinite, and merely tautology. The only speech will at last be action . . . ." (October 12, 1838)

In *Nature* Emerson solves this insoluble difficulty in various ways. Precisely as his theme is abstract and ecstatic, he holds as much as possible to the concrete circumstances of ordinary life. His tact and charm are nowhere steadier than in these references to the familiar world of commodities, institutions, workaday feeling and common talk, and in the tone resulting, the humor of an unexpectedly insistent worldliness. Here, too, the style endorses the thought. Charles Ives puts the matter well: "Emerson seems to use the great definite interests of humanity to express the greater, indefinite, spiritual values," and he stresses as Emerson's prime technical resource an "intuitive sense of values" that enabled him to "use social, political, and even economic phenomena as means of expression—as the accidental notes in his scale . . . ." The gradual change of taste in styles of prose argument effected by Romanticism and its inheritors has ratified Emerson's tactics. F. O. Matthiessen pointed out in *American Renaissance* how various touches in *Nature* (like the "pot and kettle" sentence quoted above) which were considered affected and coarse by some of his first readers, and altogether inappropriate to his dignified subject, have become the things that please us most immediately in reading him now.

But Ives is right in calling these effects accidentals. The major note is personal, elevated, and dramatic. The final message is a spoken command —"Build therefore your own world"—in a passage that turns on a forthright I-you strophe. The warmth of tone regularly invites consent, as the passing humor invites complicity. What we are made to do is not follow an argument but hear a voice, and a voice whose essential way of behaving is to project itself with full subtlety and force upon every argumentative occasion—militantly upon our inertia, sympathetically and humbly upon our doubts and fears, ironically upon conflicting pretensions, courageously ("courageous even to tenderness," Ives says) upon all that would paralyze us—so that the promise of adult health given in the last chapter of the book, the promise of "a continual self-recovery" through the "remedial force" of active spirit, is continually fulfilled on the page before us. For Emerson it was this manner of writing, self-projective, self-dramatizing, that had the best chance of being truthful. That it might also be called artful, sly, disingenuous, seems not to have worried him. By the measure of creaturely experience, artifice and insincerity had their uses, too, particularly for lofty persuasion. "There is no greater dissembler," Emerson once wrote, thinking specifically of the character of the poet, "than the sincerest man."

3. The great case of this projective and dramatic element of style in *Nature* comes in the first chapter, in that fourth paragraph the formation of which was traced on pp. xxxiv–xxxvi. The paragraph's general meaning is clear enough: by means of our vital "correspondence" with the whole of natural creation we may come into our own truest being. The governing approach, however, is to dramatize this meaning as a fact of experience, to render the idea (of a transforming sequence of exhilaration and renewal) in sentences which have a positive content of psychological, kinesthetic persuasiveness. The paragraph thus comes to a climax in an image—the self as a "transparent eye-ball" through which powerful currents "circulate"—that produces, I have always thought, the flutter of a singularly intense physical sensation. Phrase-cadence apart, "eye" would have done as well, but "eye-ball" touches to the quick. The other metaphors which Emerson combined with the metaphor of *seeing* that he thus both starts from ("few adult persons can see nature") and so remarkably returns to are more benign, yet share, several of them, this element of gross physicality: in particular the metaphor of the snake shedding its skin and that of feeding and being fed (so "daily food" indicates by just what kind of natural process "a wild delight" can subvert man's "real sorrows," and "cordial" defines substantially the species of "exhilaration" that is promised).

But to take this passage as primarily a transcription of real physical experience, and to judge its success by its power to make us believe that the moment rendered actually occurred to a particular man, is really to misconceive both its structure and the kind of truth it contains. (This is the way Jonathan Bishop appears to take it in an attentive and extremely interesting analysis that presents it as the record of an experience "of physical contact with the world" and connects its psychological details to various familiar states of "our body" and "our senses" in the condition of "physical alertness": see *Emerson on the Soul,* pp. 10–15). The passage rather seems to me conceptual in organization and, to a degree, parodistic in its language. Emerson is not necessarily writing about what demonstrably *did* happen or *will* happen at any given moment but what *might* happen according to a particular idea of the innermost nature of man —my own sense is that the passage is like most of Emerson's writing in the affirmative vein: it is fully effective only if you already know what it is meant to convey and have heard something like it before—and the whole of it continually modulates between physical images and conceptual abstractions, the predicaments of a concealed speculative thesis.

In fact the decisive leaps forward in the argument are all conceptual, or ideological. One occurs in the bare main clause, "all mean egotism vanishes," ending the vivid sentence about "standing on the bare ground,—my head bathed by the blithe air": a clause not to be found, we have already noted, in the journal entry where the sentence was first written out. In the journal this sentence ends, "I become happy in my universal relations." That is no triumph of style but it makes its point, and it would bear out the experiential theme of delight, gladness, exhilaration. ("Joy" is Bishop's word for this theme, but it is worth noting that Emerson does not in fact use the more static and Wordsworthian specification.) Why did Emerson make this particular change? For all his descriptive ebullience his concern, I will say again, is less to demonstrate the physical reality of an actual experience than to project the idea, the concept, of a certain constitutional transformation and purification possible to the self, the human ego. It is to project the idea of a *virtuous* conversion. Thus the telling qualification, "all *mean* egotism." For behind the distinction thus introduced stands, historically, the long barren struggle in the New England theology to distinguish between true and false conversion, between the self that is indeed a new being and the self that has merely come under some passing excitation of the senses, the ordinary mechanism of natural consciousness. Emerson is not interested in the old form of this doctrinal struggle, but he instinctively feels the seriousness of the issue it still poses (especially to a writer concerned to close forever the old Puritan gap between nature and grace, the creature and God); it is his burden as a New England writer to have to deal with it. "Egotism" (a word he surely could have avoided, but uses with Kantian exactness) takes this particular provincial bull by the horns; the word thus represents a raid with new philosophical weapons on an old argumentative stronghold which our time has pretty well forgotten but which Emerson's theologically minded New England audience was still mortally obsessed by.

The part played by older devotional concepts in the advance of the finished passage appears in another of these bare, unmetaphoric sentences that provide forwarding shocks—a sentence of special interest because it is the only one in the passage that Emerson would change (in fact turn completely around) in the second edition of *Nature* thirteen years later. This is the sentence, "Almost I fear to think how glad I am," that terminates the sequence, "a wild delight . . . glad . . . tribute of delight . . . good health . . . good fortune . . . a perfect exhilaration." Jonathan Bishop's analysis rightly stresses the flaunting of a paradox in this sentence, but his explanation, limited to considerations of physical feeling, is less than satisfactory. If the passage in general is to be taken seriously, something more must be involved in this intimate association of gladness and fear than "a certain anxiety as to whether the world will continue pleasing" (Bishop, p. 13). That kind of suburban anxiety would be trivial, and sentimental. What instead, describing the rush of exhilaration, the sentence literally points to is not the source of the experience in the sphere of natural feeling but the extraordinary quality it possesses in itself. It is of a fearful intensity, so "perfect" and so "wild" is the transport it brings. Emerson does not linger over this climax. In the next breath the passage turns back to ordinary nature, to "the woods" and our experience there—and there is a detectable awkwardness (registered in "too") in the transition. But the conceptual point has been made. What has come lightly to the surface here, again out of a long subtle tradition of analytic-confessional writing (and a score of Biblical texts), is the recollected idea of the immeasurable fear and trembling that are the creaturely burden of utmost revelation —and that constitute the best argument to the believer that this revelation is from, or of, "God." Emerson's later revision of this key sentence further concentrated its special emphasis. "I am glad to the brink of fear," the 1849 version reads: it is not just that the *thought* of such perfect gladness is "almost" fearful, but that the gladness itself somehow opens into a chasm of fear.

Such sentences, in any case, are not really descriptive or expository. They do not come (to cite again Bishop's careful analysis) from a "watchful" attention to real physical experience, such as may be tested by a correspondingly realistic watchfulness on the reader's part. Rather they are *projective* and *performative*. They are their own subject; they constitute an action that is itself expansive, creative of the thing referred to; they are a prose version of Romanticism's notion of a style or voice in poetry that does not merely describe familiar realities but originates new ones. The meaning they convey, the truth of the new alignment of old conceptions which they carry out, exists within this very act of discourse. To put it another way, the experience they project is grounded in a structure of ideas about experience, so that primarily what they celebrate is the suddenly revealed power and fitness of these ideas—and the fresh power of mind that, audibly parodying them in its own "other words," can thus renew them to active consciousness. The result is a mode of prose argument for which Emerson's younger contemporary Kierkegaard found the appropriate name; it is "dialectical lyric," which is the designation Kierkegaard gave to his own great study of "fear and trembling." As with so many puzzling and seemingly ill-disciplined writers of merit, so with Emerson, understanding comes more easily when we have identified the formal mode he was actually working in—and here we may recall Emerson's own regular insistence that even when writing speculatively he was fundamentally a poet.

The virtue of the whole long paragraph we are considering has to do not only with its occasional verbal pungency, its knifelike return upon its own advancing rhetoric, but also the consistency and thoroughness with which its component ideas act towards the proposed end. The projected experience of an inward conversion would not be complete or "true," for Emerson's purposes in *Nature,* if it was not shown to be convulsive of the whole being of man. Hence the extravagance of the "eyeball" sequence, which follows immediately the statement about the vanishing of "all mean egotism." Why should we suppose this extravagance was not deliberate? Why is it not a fitting rhetorical climax? The primacy of *seeing* to the whole idea of sudden and exorbitant creaturely change—note the terrible exception admitted in the parenthesis, "leaving me my eyes"—is surely reinforced by the shocking physicality of the blunt anatomical name. The eyeball *is* peculiarly sensitive (psychoanalysis has observed its special association with castration-anxiety), and the image of the self as a transparent eyeball pierced by currents of being is meant, I think, to be abruptly painful to contemplate. Elsewhere in *Nature* Emerson is soothing and benign, but at this exalted climax—as in most of the great developed passages in his work—he will not merely give comfort. The natural capacity of man is his subject, and the whole psychologically ambiguous burden of what may be in store for human beings must somehow be indicated, even if it wrenches discourse out of its ordinary tolerability.[15]

[15] Jonathan Bishop's criticism of the "eye-ball" passage makes much of the notorious caricature Emerson's friend Christopher Cranch "unerringly" chose to make of it. But Cranch, one must say, lacked literary judgment. His writing simply does not possess the critical penetration and authority of transcendentalist thinking at its best. Cranch's amusing cartoon, in any case, has little to do with the eyeball image as we reach it in context. It is rather an intramural response to the thought that the quick physical shock thus delivered has come from such an odd, kind, preacherly fellow as neighbor Emerson. Perhaps it is a charm against that shock.

It must be admitted that this whole eruptive sequence posed Emerson a further rhetorical problem. How would he return to the lower pitch of statement adopted for listing the uses of nature? It was a problem he did not really solve. The first two sentences immediately following

IV

Nature, published in September, 1836, made its mark not only in Concord and Boston. One copy went off to Carlyle in London, where, coming to the attention of men like Sterling and Monckton Milnes, it began to build the reputation that won Emerson a welcome in various Broad Church and nonconformist literary circles when he returned to England in 1848. In all, Emerson sent out about eighty presentation copies. By mid-October of 1836 he could tell his brother William that five hundred had been sold. Getting a book into print, in combination with his success at lecturing, "has bronzed me," he added, "& I am become very dogmatic." But he knew that this state of mind, in which he could identify the tenor of his own thinking with "the indisputable core of Modern History," was possible only because there were no audiences or reviewers at hand who could seriously test it: "To

---

the climactic assertion of being "part or particle of God" also have, in their brusque dismissal of friends and brothers, something naturally shocking about them (though it is Biblically sanctioned). But the various abstract assertions that finish out this long paragraph could just as well have come elsewhere in the argument—and in a different order, too, for they hardly touch one another.

such lengths of madness trot we when we have not the fear of criticism before our eyes: and the literary man in this country has no critic." Thereafter Emerson says very little about *Nature*. Its publication gave plausibility to his sense of himself as a man serving the vocation of letters, but he does not seem to think of the book as having much importance in itself. (He is more excited, more lifted up in his own self-conceived being, by the birth of his first child on October 30: "Now am I Pygmalion.") His memorable addresses at Harvard in the two succeeding years made more of an impact on public consciousness than *Nature*—in part because they had the support of his fine voice and public presence as well as of the institutional ceremonies they were composed for; in part because they were more openly controversial or, as was claimed, heretical. Certainly they had a greater effect on his reputation and subsequent career.

One may not agree with Stephen Whicher's view that *Nature* is an uncharacteristic production—"the style . . . stiff and *naïf,* the organization over-elaborate, the thought gowned in unbecoming borrowed terminology"—yet Emerson's own apparent indifference to the book after publication, and his concentration thereafter on the more congenial form of the hour-long lecture-essay, are to be noted.[16] And it is true that the ambitious scheme of the book as a whole, beginning with its title, may provoke a more particular sense of incompleteness and omission than do shorter performances on more limited topics. At several points in *Nature* the joining appears awkward and contrived (one such point, at the end of the "eye-ball" paragraph, has just been mentioned). There are other noticeable lapses. In the "Introduction" Emerson challengingly erects a critical test for new structures of thought:

"Whenever a true theory appears, it will be its own evidence. Its test is, that it will explain all phenomena. Now many are thought not only unexplained but inexplicable; as language, sleep, dreams, beasts, sex."

But we have to admit the virtual silence of *Nature* on all but the first of these "phenomena" (and on "madness," too, which was added to the list in

[16] The book was not reissued until 1849 when, slightly revised, it appeared both separately (with new pagination) and in the collection, *Nature; Addresses, and Lectures*. There were English printings in 1844, 1845, and 1848, also with other essays and lectures; all of these follow the 1836 text.

1849), a silence that is the more conspicuous if we put the book beside *Walden* and especially *Leaves of Grass*. More important, although the opening definition of "nature" includes "all other men," the main expressive context is that of unitary beings alone in a wholly physical universe: creatures of unconditioned subjectivity "embosomed for a season in nature." The social world, the great realm of "economy" that dominates the opening of *Walden,* appear only as incidental metaphors. Historical events reduce to heroic pictures showing virtue in the embrace of natural beauty; the trades and industrial labor of men indicate nothing but the spirit's abstract mastery of natural forces; "the rapid movement of the rail-road car" is only a means of introducing the eye to a new pace and rhythm of perception; ecclesiastical institutions, philosophic structures, have no more body than the original flash of spiritual insight they derive from; great centuries-old cathedrals are presented as emerging like shells, insects, and fish, out of a universal "sea of forms"; and when Caesar is mentioned, it is in the same breath and with the same rhetorical coloring as Adam. Invariably (to recall Charles Ives's comment) Emerson brings forward these allusions to the social and historical world with tact and precision, but insofar as his scheme always calls him back to considerations of the sovereign ego in unmediated relation to nature, they remain ways of speaking rather than substantial elements in the argument.

His proper subject, of course, is not "nature" in any customary sense but man, and "where & how," given the constitution we find in him, man "ought to live." Full transfer to this subject was made in Emerson's next published work, "The American Scholar." It was made, characteristically, by way of establishing a tautology—but one which served to ground his new thought, his précis of the scholar's true vocation, in the most venerable of philosophic precedents:

"He shall see that nature is the opposite of the soul, answering to it part for part. One is seal and one is print. Its beauty is the beauty of his own mind. Its laws are the laws of his own mind. Nature then becomes to him the measure of his attainments. So much of nature as he is ignorant of, so much of his own mind does he not yet possess. And, in fine, the ancient precept, "Know thyself," and the modern precept, "Study nature," become at last one maxim."

A NOTE ON THE TEXT

I

A detailed bibliographical study of the first edition of *Nature* may be found in Kenneth Walter Cameron, "Introduction," *Nature . . .*, Scholars' Facsimiles & Reprints, New York, 1940. Here we need only review Cameron's most important findings.

Nature was published anonymously on September 9 or 10, 1836, in an edition that exists in two states. In first-state copies what should be page "94" is numbered "92." In the remainder this mistake is corrected. Cameron denies that the two states constitute two distinct issues, since there are no other corrections or changes in second-state copies. This is especially noteworthy since in all copies issued in 1836 there are two obvious and closely related printer's errors of such seriousness that Emerson went to the trouble of inserting corrections in longhand in a number of copies. These occur at the beginning of "Language" (p. 32), where the omission of "spiritual" in the second "particular facts" phrase makes nonsense of proposition "2" and the pluralizing of "spirit" turns proposition "3" into something out of a theosophist's handbook.

The copy used in preparing the present edition is a first-state copy belonging to the Massachusetts Historical Society. (The Society's courtesy in allowing it to be reproduced is here acknowledged.) It is not, however, one of those with longhand corrections on p. 32.

II

Most of the corrections and revisions made for the second edition of *Nature,* in 1849, are of little importance, involving punctuation and spelling, minor changes in phrasing, the removal of the odd adverb or adjective. But in a few cases a whole sentence, or a major part of one, was recast and, most frequently, shortened. One sentence of redundant explanation was eliminated (p. 37, line 17); two new sentences were added (both in the long paragraph on p. 55). Cameron gives a full table of "verbal variants" and another table of "sentence variations" between the first and three subsequent editions, beginning with that of 1849.

Just a few of these changes are worth noting here. (Textual data resist discursive explanation; the interested reader should have a modern printing at hand to compare to the photocopy of the 1836 edition which follows.)

1. The epigraph from Plotinus, on "nature," was replaced in 1849 by a six-line verse epigraph written by Emerson himself in which the word "nature" does not appear, the argument of the poem drawing instead on several other key terms in the main text ("eye," "languages," "man," "form"). Emerson may have wanted to remove the suggestion that his book was primarily neo-Platonic in inspiration.

2. The addition of "madness" to the list of phenomena that are not yet explained (p. 7, line 6), and the very important revision of the sentence linking gladness and fear in Chapter I (p. 12, line 14), have been discussed in the Introduction.

3. The change from "part or particle of God" to "part or parcel of God" in the "eye-ball" passage in Chapter I (p. 13, line 8) is listed by Cameron for the 1849 and all subsequent editions. But the first edition of *Nature; Addresses, and Lectures,* also published in 1849, still gives "particle," a reading which is preserved in the 1892 printing of this volume by David McKay of Philadelphia for an "American Classic Series."

4. One change in "Idealism"—from "our outward being" to "the outward circumstance" (p. 70, line 12)—makes a substantial difference in meaning. It removes a possible source of confusion concerning the author's doctrine of the self but at the cost of substituting a philosophical commonplace for the psychological definiteness of the original phrase.

III

In Cameron's convenient list of verbal variants I find only one oversight: the change of tense, for the 1849 edition and after, from "I have seen" to "I see" on p. 21, line 12. This change supports the dramatic immediacy of the whole passage.

Cameron did not, however, list changes in punctuation, and some of these considerably affect the sense of the passage where they occur:

1. Two changes from full stop to semicolon (p. 29, line 5; p. 53, line 16) are chiefly in the interest of grammatical propriety but have the incidental effect of de-emphasizing a qualification which the original punctuation had made more prominent.

2. The transformation on p. 32, lines 11–15, of two grammatically parallel but separate sentences into a single sentence joined by a semicolon (the second verb being replaced by a comma) tightens the logic of the passage. So, too, does a comparable change on p. 79, line 18, rejoining the sentence about "the Supreme Being" to the long "We learn that" construction it properly follows. On the other hand the removal in lines 15–16 of two repetitions of the parallel clause-opening, "that spirit is," but without a corresponding adjustment of punctuation, weakens and even a little confuses the sense of the passage.

3. In three instances addition or subtraction of a comma alters meaning. On p. 35, line 16, a comma after "barren" changes the closing phrase, "like a single sex," from definition to illustrative simile. On p. 37, line 3, the omission in 1849 and thereafter of the original comma following the conjunction, "or," changes the function of the whole sentence; instead of making a single argumentative point in two complementary ways, it now posits some complicated and not wholly logical *either-or* situation in experience. This change would appear to contradict Emerson's main idea. On p. 41, line 16, a comma after "metaphors" notably reduces the causal dependency of the first half of the sentence upon the second and makes each half more of an independent natural truth; here, the result is more in keeping with the argument of the whole.

4. On p. 54, lines 12–13, the shift from capital letters to lower case with "Unity" and "Variety" is perhaps another gesture towards separating the book's argument from established philosophical systems. But this change was not made consistently; "Unity" remains capitalized, in 1849, through the remainder of the chapter.

5. In the second paragraph of "Idealism" a second dash, after "space," matching the dash before "deep" (p. 60, lines 6–7), rescues from confusion the force of a sentence of great importance in building this crucial passage.

6. One of the most striking revisions of all involves, again, the "eye-ball" passage (p. 13, line 8), where the full stops dividing the three short first-person declarations in the first edition were replaced in 1849 by semicolons. Full stops or periods effectively intensify the idea of a convulsive transformation, or conversion, of the entire being of man, an idea fundamental to the passage as a whole. But semicolons better act out the complementary idea of a continuous natural flow of experience. Both ideas and the feelings they convey are wanted, since both are "true" to the underlying conception. It is a case in which the ordinary conventions of print (whichever punctuation is chosen) are inadequate as indicators of meaning. Only the speaking voice could do justice to this vividly dramatic and self-projective yet precisely reasoned passage, the rhetorical mode of which, to repeat, is not descriptive or realistic but "performative."

SELECT BIBLIOGRAPHY

Besides the 1836 and 1849 editions, the essential materials for studying the composition and text of *Nature* are the following: George Willis Cooke, *A Bibliography of Ralph Waldo Emerson* (1908), which may be supplemented by Frederic I. Carpenter, *Emerson Handbook* (1953) and by various contributions to the *Emerson Society Quarterly* (1955–); *The Journals and Miscellaneous Notebooks of Ralph Waldo Emerson,* severally edited, Vols. I–V (1960–1965); *The Letters of Ralph Waldo Emerson,* ed. Ralph L. Rusk, 6 vols. (1939); *The Early Lectures of Ralph Waldo Emerson,* ed. Stephen E. Whicher and Robert E. Spiller, 2 vols. (1959, 1964).

The standard biography is Ralph L. Rusk, *The Life of Ralph Waldo Emerson* (1949), which contains a useful summary of the first reviews of *Nature*. James E. Cabot, *A Memoir of Ralph Waldo Emerson,* 2 vols. (1887), and George Edward Woodberry, *Ralph Waldo Emerson* (1907), remain valuable. Josephine Miles, *Ralph Waldo Emerson: University of Minnesota Pamphlets on American Writers, Number 41* (1964), concentrates on style and form; there is a complementary discussion of Emerson's general character as a writer in Professor Miles's *Style and Proportion* (1967), 64–78. Stephen E. Whicher, *Freedom and Fate: An Inner Life of Ralph Waldo Emerson* (1953), Sherman Paul, *Emerson's Angle of Vision* (1952), Maurice Gonnaud, *Individu et sociéte dans l'oeuvre de Ralph Waldo Emerson: essai de biographie spirituelle* (1964), and Jonathan Bishop, *Emerson on the Soul* (1964), are outstanding among recent studies; Bishop's "Notes" offer a convenient listing of important critical books and articles.

Emerson is a key figure in F. O. Matthiessen, *American Renaissance* (1941), and Charles Feidelson, Jr., *Symbolism and American Literature* (1953). *Emerson: A Collection of Critical Essays,* ed. Milton R. Konvitz and Stephen E. Whicher (1962), includes critical estimates by Robert Frost, William James, John Dewey, and George Santayana, as well as more recent academic studies by Henry Nash Smith, Henry B. Parkes, Daniel Aaron, and Newton Arvin, among others. The views of Henry James, Senior, of William James, and of Henry James, Junior, may be found in F. O. Matthiessen, *The James Family* (1948). Chapman's fine study is in *Emerson and Other Essays* (1898) and is reprinted in full in *The Shock of Recognition,* ed. Edmund Wilson (1943). Charles Ives's "Emerson" is in *Essays Before a Sonata* (1920; reprinted, with "other writings," 1964). Austin Warren, "Emerson, Preacher to Himself," *New England Saints* (1956); Kenneth Burke, "I, Eye, Ay—Concerning Emerson's Early Essay on 'Nature' and the Meaning of Transcendence," *Language as Symbolic Action* (1966); and Robert Lee Francis, "The Architectonics of Emerson's *Nature*," *American Quarterly,* XIX (Spring, 1967), are contributions to formal understanding.

The facsimile of

NATURE

NATURE.

"Nature is but an image or imitation of wisdom, the last thing of the soul; nature being a thing which doth only do, but not know."

PLOTINUS.

BOSTON:
JAMES MUNROE AND COMPANY.
M DCCC XXXVI.

Cambridge Press:
Metcalf, Torry, & Ballou.

CONTENTS.

NATURE.

CHAPTER I.

To go into solitude, a man needs to retire as much from his chamber as from society. I am not solitary whilst I read and write, though nobody is with me. But if a man would be alone, let him look at the stars. The rays that come from those heavenly worlds, will separate between him and vulgar things. One might think the atmosphere was made transparent with this design, to give man, in the heavenly bodies, the perpetual presence of the sublime. Seen in the streets of cities, how great they are! If the stars should appear one night in a thousand years, how would men believe and adore; and preserve for many generations the remembrance of the city of God which had been shown! But every night come out these preachers of beauty, and light the universe with their admonishing smile.

The stars awaken a certain reverence, because though always present, they are always inaccessible; but all natural objects make a kindred impression, when the mind is open to their influence. Nature never wears a mean appearance. Neither does the wisest man extort all her secret, and lose his curiosity by finding out all her perfection. Nature never became a toy to a wise spirit. The flowers, the animals, the mountains, reflected all the wisdom of his best hour, as much as they had delighted the simplicity of his childhood.

When we speak of nature in this manner, we have a distinct but most poetical sense in the mind. We mean the integrity of impression made by manifold natural objects. It is this which distinguishes the stick of timber of the wood-cutter, from the tree of the poet.

The charming landscape which I saw this morning, is indubitably made up of some twenty or thirty farms. Miller owns this field, Locke that, and Manning the woodland beyond. But none of them owns the landscape. There is a property in the horizon which no man has but he whose eye can integrate all the parts, that is, the poet. This is the best part of these men's farms, yet to this their land-deeds give them no title.

To speak truly, few adult persons can see nature. Most persons do not see the sun. At least they have a very superficial seeing. The sun illuminates only the eye of the man, but shines into the eye and the heart of the child. The lover of nature is he whose inward and outward senses are still truly adjusted to each other; who has retained the spirit of infancy even into the era of manhood. His intercourse with heaven and earth, becomes part of his daily food. In the presence of nature, a wild delight runs through the man, in spite of real sorrows. Nature says, — he is my creature, and maugre all his impertinent griefs, he shall be glad with me. Not the sun or the summer alone, but every hour and season yields its tribute of delight; for every hour and change corresponds to and authorizes a different state of the mind, from breathless noon to grimmest midnight. Nature is a setting that fits equally well a comic or a mourning piece. In good health, the air is a cordial of incredible virtue. Crossing a bare common, in snow puddles, at twilight, under a clouded sky, without having in my thoughts any occurrence of special good fortune, I have enjoyed a perfect exhilaration. Almost I fear to think how glad I am. In the woods too, a man casts off his years, as the snake his slough, and at what period soever of life, is always a child. In the woods, is perpetual youth. Within these plantations of God, a decorum and sanctity reign, a perennial festival is dressed, and the guest sees not how he should tire of them in a thousand years. In the woods, we return to reason and faith. There I feel that nothing can befal me in life, — no disgrace, no calamity, (leaving me my eyes,) which nature cannot repair. Standing on the bare ground, — my head bathed by the blithe air, and uplifted into infinite space, — all mean egotism vanishes. I become a transparent eye-ball. I am nothing. I see all. The currents of the Universal Being circulate through me; I am part or particle of God. The name of the nearest friend sounds then foreign and accidental. To be brothers, to be acquaintances, — master or servant, is then a trifle and a disturbance I am the lover of uncontained and immortal beauty. In the wilderness, I find something more dear and connate than in streets or villages. In the tranquil landscape, and especially in the distant line of the horizon, man beholds somewhat as beautiful as his own nature.

The greatest delight which the fields and woods minister, is the suggestion of an occult relation between man and the vegetable. I am not alone and unacknowledged. They nod to me and I to them. The waving of the boughs in the storm, is new to me and old. It takes me by surprise, and yet is not unknown. Its effect is like that of a higher thought or a better emotion coming over me, when I deemed I was thinking justly or doing right.

Yet it is certain that the power to produce this delight, does not reside in nature, but in man, or in a harmony of both. It is necessary to use these pleasures with great temperance. For, nature is not always tricked in holiday attire, but the same scene which yesterday breathed perfume and glittered as for the frolic of the nymphs, is overspread with melancholy today. Nature always wears the colors of the spirit. To a man laboring under calamity, the heat of his own fire hath sadness in it. Then, there is a kind of contempt of the landscape felt by him who has just lost by death a dear friend. The sky is less grand as it shuts down over less worth in the population.

CHAPTER II.

COMMODITY.

anything bought & sold.

WHOEVER considers the final cause of the world, will discern a multitude of uses that enter as parts into that result. They all admit of being thrown into one of the following classes; Commodity; Beauty; Language; and Discipline.

Under the general name of Commodity, I rank all those advantages which our senses owe to nature. This, of course, is a benefit which is temporary and mediate, not ultimate, like its service to the soul. Yet although low, it is perfect in its kind, and is the only use of nature which all men apprehend. The misery of man appears like childish petulance, when we explore the steady and prodigal provision that has been made for his support and delight on this green ball which floats him through the

reduce to size
you can manage
Man is huge – earth is small
Use nature as something you
can understand.

heavens. What angels invented these splendid ornaments, these rich conveniences, this ocean of air above, this ocean of water beneath, this firmament of earth between? this zodiac of lights, this tent of dropping clouds, this striped coat of climates, this fourfold year? Beasts, fire, water, stones, and corn serve him. The field is at once his floor, his work-yard, his play-ground, his garden, and his bed.

> "More servants wait on man
> Than he'll take notice of." ——

Nature, in its ministry to man, is not only the material, but is also the process and the result. All the parts incessantly work into each other's hands for the profit of man. The wind sows the seed; the sun evaporates the sea; the wind blows the vapor to the field; the ice, on the other side of the planet, condenses rain on this; the rain feeds the plant; the plant feeds the animal; and thus the endless circulations of the divine charity nourish man.

The useful arts are but reproductions or new combinations by the wit of man, of the same natural benefactors. He no longer waits for favoring gales, but by means of steam, he realizes the fable of Æolus's bag, and carries the two and thirty winds in the boiler of his boat. To diminish friction, he paves the road with iron bars, and, mounting a coach with a ship-load of men, animals, and merchandise behind him, he darts through the country, from town to town, like an eagle or a swallow through the air. By the aggregate of these aids, how is the face of the world changed, from the era of Noah to that of Napoleon! The private poor man hath cities, ships, canals, bridges, built for him. He goes to the post-office, and the human race run on his errands; to the book-shop, and the human race read and write of all that happens, for him; to the court-house, and nations repair his wrongs. He sets his house upon the road, and the human race go forth every morning, and shovel out the snow, and cut a path for him.

But there is no need of specifying particulars in this class of uses. The catalogue is endless, and the examples so obvious, that I shall leave them to the reader's reflection, with the general remark, that this mercenary benefit is one which has respect to a farther good. A man is fed, not that he may be fed, but that he may work.

CHAPTER III.

BEAUTY.

A NOBLER want of man is served by nature, namely, the love of Beauty.

The ancient Greeks called the world κοσμος, beauty. Such is the constitution of all things, or such the plastic power of the human eye, that the primary forms, as the sky, the mountain, the tree, the animal, give us a delight *in and for themselves;* a pleasure arising from outline, color, motion, and grouping. This seems partly owing to the eye itself. The eye is the best of artists. By the mutual action of its structure and of the laws of light, perspective is produced, which integrates every mass of objects, of what character soever, into a well colored and shaded globe, so that where the particular objects are mean and unaffecting, the landscape which they compose, is round and symmetrical. And as the eye is the best composer, so light is the first of painters. There is no object so foul that intense light will not make beautiful. And the stimulus it affords to the sense, and a sort of infinitude which it hath, like space and time, make all matter gay. Even the corpse hath its own beauty. But beside this general grace diffused over nature, almost all the individual forms are agreeable to the eye, as is proved by our endless imitations of some of them, as the acorn, the grape, the pine-cone, the wheat-ear, the egg, the wings and forms of most birds, the lion's claw, the serpent, the butterfly, sea-shells, flames, clouds, buds, leaves, and the forms of many trees, as the palm.

For better consideration, we may distribute the aspects of Beauty in a threefold manner.

1. First, the simple perception of natural forms is a delight. The influence of the forms and actions in nature, is so needful to man, that, in its lowest functions, it seems to lie on the confines of commodity and beauty. To the body and mind

which have been cramped by noxious work or company, nature is medicinal and restores their tone. The tradesman, the attorney comes out of the din and craft of the street, and sees the sky and the woods, and is a man again. In their eternal calm, he finds himself. The health of the eye seems to demand a horizon. We are never tired, so long as we can see far enough.

But in other hours, Nature satisfies the soul purely by its loveliness, and without any mixture of corporeal benefit. I have seen the spectacle of morning from the hill-top over against my house, from day-break to sun-rise, with emotions which an angel might share. The long slender bars of cloud float like fishes in the sea of crimson light. From the earth, as a shore, I look out into that silent sea. I seem to partake its rapid transformations: the active enchantment reaches my dust, and I dilate and conspire with the morning wind. How does Nature deify us with a few and cheap elements! Give me health and a day, and I will make the pomp of emperors ridiculous. The dawn is my Assyria; the sun-set and moon-rise my Paphos, and unimaginable realms of faerie; broad noon shall be my England of the senses and the understanding; the night shall be my Germany of mystic philosophy and dreams.

Not less excellent, except for our less susceptibility in the afternoon, was the charm, last evening, of a January sunset. The western clouds divided and subdivided themselves into pink flakes modulated with tints of unspeakable softness; and the air had so much life and sweetness, that it was a pain to come within doors. What was it that nature would say? Was there no meaning in the live repose of the valley behind the mill, and which Homer or Shakspeare could not re-form for me in words? The leafless trees become spires of flame in the sunset, with the blue east for their background, and the stars of the dead calices of flowers, and every withered stem and stubble rimed with frost, contribute something to the mute music.

The inhabitants of cities suppose that the country landscape is pleasant only half the year. I please myself with observing the graces of the winter scenery, and believe that we are as much touched by it as by the genial influences of summer. To the attentive eye, each moment of the year has its own beauty, and in the same field, it beholds, every hour, a picture which was never seen before, and which shall never be seen again. The heavens change every moment, and reflect their glory or gloom on the plains beneath. The state of the crop in the surrounding farms alters the expression of the earth from week to week. The succession of native plants in the pastures and roadsides, which make the silent clock by which time tells the summer hours, will make even the divisions of the day sensible to a keen observer. The tribes of birds and insects, like the plants punctual to their time, follow each other, and the year has room for all. By watercourses, the variety is greater. In July, the blue pontederia or pickerel-weed blooms in large beds in the shallow parts of our pleasant river, and swarms with yellow butterflies in continual motion. Art cannot rival this pomp of purple and gold. Indeed the river is a perpetual gala, and boasts each month a new ornament.

But this beauty of Nature which is seen and felt as beauty, is the least part. The shows of day, the dewy morning, the rainbow, mountains, orchards in blossom, stars, moonlight, shadows in still water, and the like, if too eagerly hunted, become shows merely, and mock us with their unreality. Go out of the house to see the moon, and 't is mere tinsel; it will not please as when its light shines upon your necessary journey. The beauty that shimmers in the yellow afternoons of October, who ever could clutch it? Go forth to find it, and it is gone: 't is only a mirage as you look from the windows of diligence.

2. The presence of a higher, namely, of the spiritual element is essential to its perfection. The high and divine beauty which can be loved

strong argument - beauty accompanies virtuous acts - M - Billy Budd without effeminacy, is that which is found in combination with the human will, and never separate. Beauty is the mark God sets upon virtue. Every natural action is graceful. Every heroic act is also decent, and causes the place and the bystanders to shine. We are taught by great actions that the universe is the property of every individual in it. Every rational creature has all nature for his dowry and estate. It is his, if he will. He may divest himself of it; he may creep into a corner, and abdicate his kingdom, as most men do, but he is entitled to the world by his constitution. In proportion to the energy of his thought and will, he takes up the world into himself. "All those things for which men plough, build, or sail, obey virtue;" said an ancient historian. "The winds and waves," said Gibbon, "are always on the side of the ablest navigators." So are the sun and moon and all the stars of heaven. When a noble act is done,—perchance in a scene of great natural beauty; when Leonidas and his three hundred martyrs consume one day in dying, and the sun and moon come each and look at them once in the steep defile of Thermopylæ; when Arnold Winkelried, in the high Alps, under the shadow of the avalanche, gathers in his side a sheaf of Austrian spears to break the line for his comrades; are not these heroes entitled to add the beauty of the scene to the beauty of the deed? When the bark of Columbus nears the shore of America; — before it, the beach lined with savages, fleeing out of all their huts of cane; the sea behind; and the purple mountains of the Indian Archipelago around, can we separate the man from the living picture? Does not the New World clothe his form with her palm-groves and savannahs as fit drapery? Ever does natural beauty steal in like air, and envelope great actions. When Sir Harry Vane was dragged up the Tower-hill, sitting on a sled, to suffer death, as the champion of the English laws, one of the multitude cried out to him, "You never sate on so glorious a seat." Charles II., to intimidate the citizens of London, caused the patriot Lord Russel to be drawn in an open coach, through the principal streets of the city, on his way to the scaffold. "But," to use the simple narrative of his biographer, "the multitude imagined they saw liberty and virtue sitting by his side." In private places, among sordid objects, an act of truth or heroism seems at once to draw to itself the sky as its temple, the sun as its candle. Nature stretcheth out her arms to embrace man, only let his thoughts be of equal greatness. Willingly does she follow his steps with the rose and the violet, and bend her lines of grandeur and grace to the decoration of her darling child. Only let his thoughts be of equal scope, and the frame will suit the picture. A virtuous man, is in unison with her works, and makes the central figure of the visible sphere. Homer, Pindar, Socrates, Phocion, associate themselves fitly in our memory with the whole geography and climate of Greece. The visible heavens and earth sympathize with Jesus. And in common life, whosoever has seen a person of powerful character and happy genius, will have remarked how easily he took all things along with him, — the persons, the opinions, and the day, and nature became ancillary to a man.

3. There is still another aspect under which the beauty of the world may be viewed, namely, as it becomes an object of the intellect. Beside the relation of things to virtue, they have a relation to thought. The intellect searches out the absolute order of things as they stand in the mind of God, and without the colors of affection. The intellectual and the active powers seem to succeed each other in man, and the exclusive activity of the one, generates the exclusive activity of the other. There is something unfriendly in each to the other, but they are like the alternate periods of feeding and working in animals; each prepares and certainly will be followed by the other. Therefore does beauty, which, in relation to actions, as we have seen comes unsought, and comes because it is unsought, remain for the apprehension and pursuit of the intellect; and then again, in its turn, of the active power. Nothing divine dies. All

good is eternally reproductive. The beauty of nature reforms itself in the mind, and not for barren contemplation, but for new creation.

All men are in some degree impressed by the face of the world. Some men even to delight. This love of beauty is Taste. Others have the same love in such excess, that, not content with admiring, they seek to embody it in new forms. The creation of beauty is Art.

The production of a work of art throws a light upon the mystery of humanity. A work of art is an abstract or epitome of the world. It is the result or expression of nature, in miniature. For although the works of nature are innumerable and all different, the result or the expression of them all is similar and single. Nature is a sea of forms radically alike and even unique. A leaf, a sun-beam, a landscape, the ocean, make an analogous impression on the mind. What is common to them all,—that perfectness and harmony, is beauty. Therefore the standard of beauty, is the entire circuit of natural forms,—the totality of nature;

which the Italians expressed by defining beauty "il piu nell' uno." Nothing is quite beautiful alone: nothing but is beautiful in the whole. A single object is only so far beautiful as it suggests this universal grace. The poet, the painter, the sculptor, the musician, the architect seek each to concentrate this radiance of the world on one point, and each in his several work to satisfy the love of beauty which stimulates him to produce. Thus is Art, a nature passed through the alembic of man. Thus in art, does nature work through the will of a man filled with the beauty of her first works.

The world thus exists to the soul to satisfy the desire of beauty. Extend this element to the uttermost, and I call it an ultimate end. No reason can be asked or given why the soul seeks beauty. Beauty, in its largest and profoundest sense, is one expression for the universe. God is the all-fair. Truth, and goodness, and beauty, are but different faces of the same All. But beauty in nature is not ultimate. It is the herald of inward and eternal beauty, and is not alone a solid and satisfactory good. It must therefore stand as a part and not as yet the last or highest expression of the final cause of Nature.

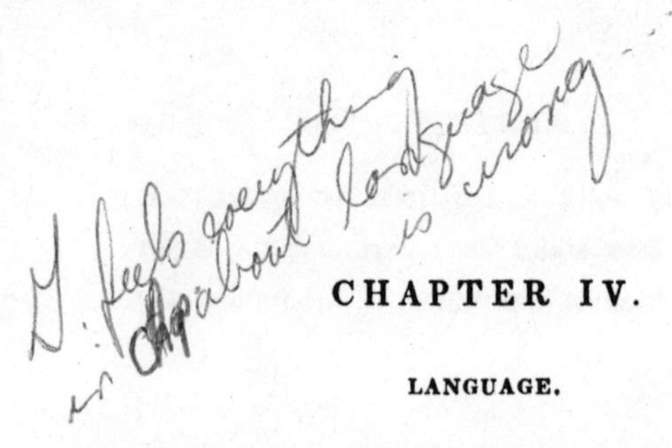

CHAPTER IV.

LANGUAGE.

A THIRD use which Nature subserves to man is that of Language. Nature is the vehicle of thought, and in a simple, double, and threefold degree.

1. Words are signs of natural facts.

2. Particular natural facts are symbols of particular facts.

3. Nature is the symbol of spirits.

1. Words are signs of natural facts. The use of natural history is to give us aid in supernatural history. The use of the outer creation is to give us language for the beings and changes of the inward creation. Every word which is used to express a moral or intellectual fact, if traced to its root, is found to be borrowed from some material appearance. *Right* originally means *straight; wrong* means *twisted. Spirit* primarily means *wind; trans-*

gression, the crossing of a *line; supercilious*, the *raising of the eye-brow*. We say the *heart* to express emotion, the *head* to denote thought; and *thought* and *emotion* are, in their turn, words borrowed from sensible things, and now appropriated to spiritual nature. Most of the process by which this transformation is made, is hidden from us in the remote time when language was framed; but the same tendency may be daily observed in children. Children and savages use only nouns or names of things, which they continually convert into verbs, and apply to analogous mental acts.

2. But this origin of all words that convey a spiritual import, — so conspicuous a fact in the history of language, — is our least debt to nature. It is not words only that are emblematic; it is things which are emblematic. Every natural fact is a symbol of some spiritual fact. Every appearance in nature corresponds to some state of the mind, and that state of the mind can only be described by presenting that natural appearance as its picture. An enraged

man is a lion, a cunning man is a fox, a firm man is a rock, a learned man is a torch. A lamb is innocence; a snake is subtle spite; flowers express to us the delicate affections. Light and darkness are our familiar expression for knowledge and ignorance; and heat for love. Visible distance behind and before us, is respectively our image of memory and hope.

Who looks upon a river in a meditative hour, and is not reminded of the flux of all things? Throw a stone into the stream, and the circles that propagate themselves are the beautiful type of all influence. Man is conscious of a universal soul within or behind his individual life, wherein, as in a firmament, the natures of Justice, Truth, Love, Freedom, arise and shine. This universal soul, he calls Reason: it is not mine or thine or his, but we are its; we are its property and men. And the blue sky in which the private earth is buried, the sky with its eternal calm, and full of everlasting orbs, is the type of Reason. That which, intellectually considered, we call Reason, considered in relation to nature, we call Spirit. Spirit is the Creator. Spirit hath life in itself. And man in all ages and countries, embodies it in his language, as the FATHER.

It is easily seen that there is nothing lucky or capricious in these analogies, but that they are constant, and pervade nature. These are not the dreams of a few poets, here and there, but man is an analogist, and studies relations in all objects. He is placed in the centre of beings, and a ray of relation passes from every other being to him. And neither can man be understood without these objects, nor these objects without man. All the facts in natural history taken by themselves, have no value, but are barren like a single sex. But marry it to human history, and it is full of life. Whole Floras, all Linnæus' and Buffon's volumes, are but dry catalogues of facts; but the most trivial of these facts, the habit of a plant, the organs, or work, or noise of an insect, applied to the illustration of a fact in intellectual philosophy, or, in any way associated to human nature, affects us in the most lively and agreeable manner. The seed of a plant, — to what affecting analogies in the nature of man, is that little fruit made use of, in all discourse, up to the voice of Paul, who calls the human corpse a seed, — "It is sown a natural body; it is raised a spiritual body." The motion of the earth round its axis, and round the sun, makes the day, and the year. These are certain amounts of brute light and heat. But is there no intent of an analogy between man's life and the seasons? And do the seasons gain no grandeur or pathos from that analogy? The instincts of the ant are very unimportant considered as the ant's; but the moment a ray of relation is seen to ex tend from it to man, and the little drudge is seen to be a monitor, a little body with a mighty heart, then all its habits, even that said to be recently observed, that it never sleeps, become sublime.

Because of this radical correspondence between visible things and human thoughts, savages, who have only what is necessary, converse in figures. As we go back in history, language becomes more picturesque, until its infancy, when it is all poetry; or, all spiritual facts are represented by natural symbols. The same symbols are found to make the original elements of all languages. It has moreover been observed, that the idioms of all languages approach each other in passages of the greatest eloquence and power. And as this is the first language, so is it the last. This immediate dependence of language upon nature, this conversion of an outward phenomenon into a type of somewhat in human life, never loses its power to affect us. It is this which gives that piquancy to the conversation of a strong-natured farmer or back-woodsman, which all men relish.

Thus is nature an interpreter, by whose means man converses with his fellow men. A man's power to connect his thought with its proper symbol, and so utter it, depends on the simplicity of his character, that is, upon his love of truth and his desire to communicate it without loss. The corruption of man is followed by the corruption of language. When simplicity of character and the sovereignty of ideas is broken up by the prevalence of secondary desires, the desire of riches, the desire of pleasure, the desire of power, the desire of praise, — and duplicity and falsehood take place of simplicity and truth, the power over nature as an interpreter of the will, is in a degree lost; new imagery ceases to be created, and old words are perverted to stand for things which are not; a paper currency is employed when there is no bullion in the vaults. In due time, the fraud is manifest, and words lose all power to stimulate the understanding or the affections. Hundreds of writers may be found in every long-civilized nation, who for a short time believe, and make others believe, that they see and utter truths, who do not of themselves clothe one thought in its natural garment, but who feed unconsciously upon the language created by the primary writers of the country, those, namely, who hold primarily on nature.

But wise men pierce this rotten diction and fasten words again to visible things; so that picturesque language is at once a commanding certificate that he who employs it, is a man in alliance with truth and God. The moment our discourse rises above the ground line of familiar facts, and is inflamed with passion or exalted by thought, it clothes itself in images. A man conversing in earnest, if he watch his intellectual processes, will find that always a material image, more or less luminous, arises in his mind, cotemporaneous with every thought, which furnishes the vestment of the thought. Hence, good writing and brilliant discourse are perpetual allegories. This imagery is spontaneous. It is the blending of experience with the present action of the mind. It is proper creation. It is the working of the Original Cause through the instruments he has already made.

These facts may suggest the advantage which the country-life possesses for a powerful mind, over the artificial and curtailed life of cities. We know more from nature than we can at will communicate. Its light flows into the mind evermore, and we forget its presence. The poet, the orator, bred in the woods, whose senses have been nourished by their fair and appeasing changes, year after year, without design and without heed, — shall not lose their lesson altogether, in the roar of cities or the broil of politics. Long hereafter, amidst agitation and terror in national councils, — in the hour of revolution, — these solemn images shall reappear in their morning lustre, as fit symbols and words of the thoughts which the passing events shall awaken. At the call of a noble sentiment, again the woods wave, the pines murmur, the river rolls and shines, and the cattle low upon the mountains, as he saw and heard them in his infancy. And with these forms, the spells of persuasion, the keys of power are put into his hands.

3. We are thus assisted by natural objects in the expression of particular meanings. But how great a language to convey such peppercorn informations! Did it need such noble

races of creatures, this profusion of forms, this host of orbs in heaven, to furnish man with the dictionary and grammar of his municipal speech? Whilst we use this grand cipher to expedite the affairs of our pot and kettle, we feel that we have not yet put it to its use, neither are able. We are like travellers using the cinders of a volcano to roast their eggs. Whilst we see that it always stands ready to clothe what we would say, we cannot avoid the question, whether the characters are not significant of themselves. Have mountains, and waves, and skies, no significance but what we consciously give them, when we employ them as emblems of our thoughts? The world is emblematic. Parts of speech are metaphors because the whole of nature is a metaphor of the human mind. The laws of moral nature answer to those of matter as face to face in a glass. "The visible world and the relation of its parts, is the dial plate of the invisible." The axioms of physics translate the laws of ethics. Thus, "the whole is greater than its part;" "reaction is equal to action;" "the smallest weight may be made to lift the greatest, the difference of weight being compensated by time;" and many the like propositions, which have an ethical as well as physical sense. These propositions have a much more extensive and universal sense when applied to human life, than when confined to technical use.

In like manner, the memorable words of history, and the proverbs of nations, consist usually of a natural fact, selected as a picture or parable of a moral truth. Thus; A rolling stone gathers no moss; A bird in the hand is worth two in the bush; A cripple in the right way, will beat a racer in the wrong; Make hay whilst the sun shines; 'T is hard to carry a full cup even; Vinegar is the son of wine; The last ounce broke the camel's back; Long-lived trees make roots first; — and the like. In their primary sense these are trivial facts, but we repeat them for the value of their analogical import. What is true of proverbs, is true of all fables, parables, and allegories.

This relation between the mind and matter is not fancied by some poet, but stands in the will of God, and so is free to be known by all men. It appears to men, or it does not appear. When in fortunate hours we ponder this miracle, the wise man doubts, if, at all other times, he is not blind and deaf;

> —— "Can these things be,
> And overcome us like a summer's cloud,
> Without our special wonder?"

for the universe becomes transparent, and the light of higher laws than its own, shines through it. It is the standing problem which has exercised the wonder and the study of every fine genius since the world began; from the era of the Egyptians and the Brahmins, to that of Pythagoras, of Plato, of Bacon, of Leibnitz, of Swedenborg. There sits the Sphinx at the road-side, and from age to age, as each prophet comes by, he tries his fortune at reading her riddle. There seems to be a necessity in spirit to manifest itself in material forms; and day and night, river and storm, beast and bird, acid and alkali, preëxist in necessary Ideas in the mind of God, and are what they are by virtue of preceding affections, in the world of spirit. A Fact is the end or last issue of spirit. The visible creation is the terminus or the circumference of the invisible world. "Material objects," said a French philosopher, "are necessarily kinds of *scoriæ* of the substantial thoughts of the Creator, which must always preserve an exact relation to their first origin; in other words, visible nature must have a spiritual and moral side."

This doctrine is abstruse, and though the images of "garment," "scoriæ," "mirror," &c., may stimulate the fancy, we must summon the aid of subtler and more vital expositors to make it plain. "Every scripture is to be interpreted by the same spirit which gave it forth," — is the fundamental law of criticism. A life in harmony with nature, the love of truth and of virtue, will purge the eyes to understand her text. By degrees we may come to know the primitive sense of the permanent objects of nature, so that the world shall be to us an open book, and every form significant of its hidden life and final cause.

A new interest surprises us, whilst, under the view now suggested, we contemplate the fearful extent and multitude of objects; since "every object rightly seen, unlocks a new faculty of the soul." That which was unconscious truth, becomes, when interpreted and defined in an object, a part of the domain of knowledge, — a new amount to the magazine of power.

CHAPTER V.

DISCIPLINE.

In view of this significance of nature, we arrive at once at a new fact, that nature is a discipline. This use of the world includes the preceding uses, as parts of itself.

Space, time, society, labor, climate, food, locomotion, the animals, the mechanical forces, give us sincerest lessons, day by day, whose meaning is unlimited. They educate both the Understanding and the Reason. Every property of matter is a school for the understanding, — its solidity or resistance, its inertia, its extension, its figure, its divisibility. The understanding adds, divides, combines, measures, and finds everlasting nutriment and room for its activity in this worthy scene. Meantime, Reason transfers all these lessons into its own world of thought, by perceiving the analogy that marries Matter and Mind.

1. Nature is a discipline of the understanding in intellectual truths. Our dealing with sensible objects is a constant exercise in the necessary lessons of difference, of likeness, of order, of being and seeming, of progressive arrangement; of ascent from particular to general; of combination to one end of manifold forces. Proportioned to the importance of the organ to be formed, is the extreme care with which its tuition is provided,—a care pretermitted in no single case. What tedious training, day after day, year after year, never ending, to form the common sense; what continual reproduction of annoyances, inconveniences, dilemmas; what rejoicing over us of little men; what disputing of prices, what reckonings of interest,—and all to form the Hand of the mind;—to instruct us that "good thoughts are no better than good dreams, unless they be executed!"

The same good office is performed by Property and its filial systems of debt and credit. Debt, grinding debt, whose iron face the widow, the orphan, and the sons of genius fear and hate; — debt, which consumes so much time, which so cripples and disheartens a great spirit with cares that seem so base, is a preceptor whose lessons cannot be forgone, and is needed most by those who suffer from it most. Moreover, property, which has been well compared to snow, — "if it fall level to-day, it will be blown into drifts to-morrow," — is merely the surface action of internal machinery, like the index on the face of a clock. Whilst now it is the gymnastics of the understanding, it is hiving in the foresight of the spirit, experience in profounder laws.

The whole character and fortune of the individual is affected by the least inequalities in the culture of the understanding; for example, in the perception of differences. Therefore is Space, and therefore Time, that man may know that things are not huddled and lumped, but sundered and individual. A bell and a plough have each their use, and neither can do the office of the other. Water is good to drink, coal to burn, wool to wear; but wool cannot be drunk, nor water spun, nor coal eaten. The wise man shows his wisdom in separation, in gradation, and his scale of creatures and of merits, is as wide as nature. The foolish have no range in their scale, but suppose every man is as every other man. What is not good they call the worst, and what is not hateful, they call the best.

In like manner, what good heed, nature forms in us! She pardons no mistakes. Her yea is yea, and her nay, nay.

The first steps in Agriculture, Astronomy, Zoölogy, (those first steps which the farmer, the hunter, and the sailor take,) teach that nature's dice are always loaded; that in her heaps and rubbish are concealed sure and useful results.

How calmly and genially the mind apprehends one after another the laws of physics! What noble emotions dilate the mortal as he enters into the counsels of the creation, and feels by knowledge the privilege to BE! His insight refines him. The beauty of nature shines in his own breast. Man is greater that he can see this, and the universe less, because Time and Space relations vanish as laws are known.

Here again we are impressed and even daunted by the immense Universe to be explored. 'What we know, is a point to what we do not know.' Open any recent journal of science, and weigh the problems suggested concerning Light, Heat, Electricity, Magnetism, Physiology, Geology, and judge whether the interest of natural science is likely to be soon exhausted.

Passing by many particulars of the discipline of nature we must not omit to specify two.

The exercise of the Will or the lesson of power is taught in every event. From the child's successive possession of his several senses up to the hour when he saith, "thy will be done!" he is learning the secret, that he can reduce under his will, not only particular events, but great classes, nay the whole series of events, and so conform all facts to his character. Nature is thoroughly mediate. It is made to serve. It receives the dominion of man as meekly as the ass on which the Saviour rode. It offers all its kingdoms to man as the raw material which he may mould into what is useful. Man is never weary of working it up. He forges the subtile and delicate air into wise and melodious words, and gives them wing as angels of persuasion and command. More and more, with every thought, does his kingdom stretch over things, until the world becomes, at last, only a realized will, — the double of the man.

2. Sensible objects conform to the premonitions of Reason and reflect the conscience. All things are moral; and in their boundless changes have an unceasing reference to spiritual nature. Therefore is nature glorious with form, color, and motion, that every globe in the remotest heaven; every chemical change from the rudest crystal up to the laws of life; every change of vegetation from the first principle of growth in the eye of a leaf, to the tropical forest and antediluvian coal-mine; every animal function from the sponge up to Hercules, shall hint or thunder to man the laws of right and wrong, and echo the Ten Commandments. Therefore

is nature always the ally of Religion: lends all her pomp and riches to the religious sentiment. Prophet and priest, David, Isaiah, Jesus, have drawn deeply from this source.

This ethical character so penetrates the bone and marrow of nature, as to seem the end for which it was made. Whatever private purpose is answered by any member or part, this is its public and universal function, and is never omitted. Nothing in nature is exhausted in its first use. When a thing has served an end to the uttermost, it is wholly new for an ulterior service. In God, every end is converted into a new means. Thus the use of Commodity, regarded by itself, is mean and squalid. But it is to the mind an education in the great doctrine of Use, namely, that a thing is good only so far as it serves; that a conspiring of parts and efforts to the production of an end, is essential to any being. The first and gross manifestation of this truth, is our inevitable and hated training in values and wants, in corn and meat.

It has already been illustrated, in treating of the significance of material things, that every natural process is but a version of a moral sentence. The moral law lies at the centre of nature and radiates to the circumference. It is the pith and marrow of every substance, every relation, and every process. All things with which we deal, preach to us. What is a farm but a mute gospel? The chaff and the wheat, weeds and plants, blight, rain, insects, sun, — it is a sacred emblem from the first furrow of spring to the last stack which the snow of winter overtakes in the fields. But the sailor, the shepherd, the miner, the merchant, in their several resorts, have each an experience precisely parallel and leading to the same conclusions. Because all organizations are radically alike. Nor can it be doubted that this moral sentiment which thus scents the air, and grows in the grain, and impregnates the waters of the world, is caught by man and sinks into his soul. The moral influence of nature upon every individual is that amount of truth which it illustrates to him.

Who can estimate this? Who can guess how much firmness the sea-beaten rock has taught the fisherman? how much tranquillity has been reflected to man from the azure sky, over whose unspotted deeps the winds forevermore drive flocks of stormy clouds, and leave no wrinkle or stain? how much industry and providence and affection we have caught from the pantomime of brutes? What a searching preacher of self-command is the varying phenomenon of Health!

Herein is especially apprehended the Unity of Nature, — the Unity in Variety, — which meets us everywhere. All the endless variety of things make a unique, an identical impression. Xenophanes complained in his old age, that, look where he would, all things hastened back to Unity. He was weary of seeing the same entity in the tedious variety of forms. The fable of Proteus has a cordial truth. Every particular in nature, a leaf, a drop, a crystal, a moment of time is related to the whole, and partakes of the perfection of the whole. Each particle is a microcosm, and faithfully renders the likeness of the world.

Not only resemblances exist in things whose analogy is obvious, as when we detect the type of the human hand in the flipper of the fossil saurus, but also in objects wherein there is great superficial unlikeness. Thus architecture is called 'frozen music,' by De Stael and Goethe. 'A Gothic church,' said Coleridge, 'is a petrified religion.' Michael Angelo maintained, that, to an architect, a knowledge of anatomy is essential. In Haydn's oratorios, the notes present to the imagination not only motions, as, of the snake, the stag, and the elephant, but colors also; as the green grass. The granite is differenced in its laws only by the more or less of heat, from the river that wears it away. The river, as it flows, resembles the air that flows over it; the air resembles the light which traverses it with more subtile currents; the light resembles the heat which rides with it through Space. Each creature is only a modification of the other; the likeness in them is more than the difference, and their radical law is one and the same. Hence it is, that a rule of one art, or a law of one organization, holds true throughout nature. So intimate is this Unity, that, it is easily seen, it lies under the undermost garment of nature, and betrays its source in universal Spirit. For, it pervades Thought also. Every universal truth which we express in words, implies or supposes every other truth. *Omne verum vero consonat*. It is like a great circle on a sphere, comprising all possible circles; which, however, may be drawn, and comprise it, in like manner. Every such truth is the absolute Ens seen from one side. But it has innumerable sides.

The same central Unity is still more conspicuous in actions. Words are finite organs of the infinite mind. They cannot cover the dimensions of what is in truth. They break, chop, and impoverish it. An action is the perfection and publication of thought. A right action seems to fill the eye, and to be related to all nature. "The wise man, in doing one thing, does all; or, in the one thing he does rightly, he sees the likeness of all which is [illegible] ..ly."

Words and actions are not the attributes of mute and brute nature. They introduce us to that singular form which predominates over all other forms. This is the human. All other organizations appear to be degradations of the human form. When this organization appears among so many that surround it, the spirit prefers it to all others. It says, 'From such as this, have I drawn joy and knowledge. In such as this, have I found and beheld myself. I will speak to it. It can speak again. It can yield me thought already formed and alive.' In fact, the eye, — the mind, — is always accompanied by these forms, male and female; and these are incomparably the richest informations of the power and order that lie at the heart of things. Unfortunately, every one of them bears the marks as of some injury; is marred and superficially defective. Nevertheless, far different from the deaf and dumb nature around them, these all rest like fountain-pipes on the unfathomed sea of thought and virtue whereto they alone, of all organizations, are the entrances.

It were a pleasant inquiry to follow into detail their ministry to our education, but where would it stop? We are associated in adolescent and adult life with some friends, who, like skies and waters, are coextensive with our idea; who, answering each to a certain affection of the soul, satisfy our desire on that side; whom we lack power to put at such focal distance from us, that we can mend or even analyze them. We cannot chuse but love them. When much intercourse with a friend has supplied us with a standard of excellence, and has increased our respect for the resources of God who thus sends a real person to outgo our ideal; when he has, moreover, become an object of thought, and, whilst his character retains all its unconscious effect, is converted in the mind into solid and sweet wisdom, — it is a sign to us that his office is closing, and he is commonly withdrawn from our sight in a short time.

CHAPTER VI.

IDEALISM.

Thus is the unspeakable but intelligible and practicable meaning of the world conveyed to man, the immortal pupil, in every object of sense. To this one end of Discipline, all parts of nature conspire.

A noble doubt perpetually suggests itself, whether this end be not the Final Cause of the Universe; and whether nature outwardly exists. It is a sufficient account of that Appearance we call the World, that God will teach a human mind, and so makes it the receiver of a certain number of congruent sensations, which we call sun and moon, man and woman, house and trade. In my utter impotence to test the authenticity of the report of my senses, to know whether the impressions they make on me correspond with outlying objects, what difference does it make, whether Orion is up there in heaven, or some god paints the image in the firmament of the soul? The relations of parts and the end of the whole remaining the same, what is the difference, whether land and sea interact, and worlds revolve and intermingle without number or end, — deep yawning under deep, and galaxy balancing galaxy, throughout absolute space, or, whether, without relations of time and space, the same appearances are inscribed in the constant faith of man. Whether nature enjoy a substantial existence without, or is only in the apocalypse of the mind, it is alike useful and alike venerable to me. Be it what it may, it is ideal to me, so long as I cannot try the accuracy of my senses.

The frivolous make themselves merry with the Ideal theory, as if its consequences were burlesque; as if it affected the stability of nature. It surely does not. God never jests with us, and will not compromise the end of nature, by permitting any inconsequence in its procession. Any distrust of the permanence of laws, would paralyze the faculties of man. Their permanence is sacredly respected, and his faith therein is perfect. The wheels and springs of man are all set to the hypothesis of the permanence of nature. We are not built like a ship to be tossed, but like a house to stand. It is a natural consequence of this structure, that, so long as the active powers predominate over the reflective, we resist with indignation any hint that nature is more short-lived or mutable than spirit. The broker, the wheelwright, the carpenter, the tollman, are much displeased at the intimation.

But whilst we acquiesce entirely in the permanence of natural laws, the question of the absolute existence of nature, still remains open. It is the uniform effect of culture on the human mind, not to shake our faith in the stability of particular phenomena, as of heat, water, azote; but to lead us to regard nature as a phenomenon, not a substance; to attribute necessary existence to spirit; to esteem nature as an accident and an effect.

To the senses and the unrenewed understanding, belongs a sort of instinctive belief in the absolute existence of nature. In their view, man and nature are indissolubly joined. Things are ultimates, and they never look beyond their sphere. The presence of Reason mars this faith. The first effort of thought tends to relax this despotism of the senses, which binds us to nature as if we were a part of it, and shows us nature aloof, and, as it were, afloat. Until this higher agency intervened, the animal eye sees, with wonderful accuracy, sharp outlines and colored surfaces. When the eye of Reason opens, to outline and surface are at once added, grace and expression. These proceed from imagination and affection, and abate somewhat of the angular distinctness of objects. If the Reason be stimulated to more earnest vision, outlines and surfaces become transparent, and are no longer seen ; causes and spirits are seen through them. The best, the happiest moments of life, are these delicious awakenings of the higher powers, and the reverential withdrawing of nature before its God.

Let us proceed to indicate the effects of culture. 1. Our first institution in the Ideal philosophy is a hint from nature herself.

Nature is made to conspire with spirit to emancipate us. Certain mechanical changes, a small alteration in our local position apprizes us of a dualism. We are strangely affected by seeing the shore from a moving ship, from a balloon, or through the tints of an unusual sky. The least change in our point of view, gives the whole world a pictorial air. A man who seldom rides, needs only to get into a coach and traverse his own town, to turn the street into a puppet-show. The men, the women, — talking, running, bartering, fighting, — the earnest mechanic, the lounger, the beggar, the boys, the dogs, are unrealized at once, or, at least, wholly detached from all relation to the observer, and seen as apparent, not substantial beings. What new thoughts are suggested by seeing a face of country quite familiar, in the rapid movement of the rail-road car! Nay, the most wonted objects, (make a very slight change in the point of vission,) please us most. In a camera obscura, the butcher's cart, and the figure of one of our own family amuse us. So a protrait of a well-known face gratifies us. Turn the eyes upside down, by looking at the landscape through your legs, and how agreeable is the picture, though you have seen it any time these twenty years!

In these cases, by mechanical means, is suggested the difference between the observer and the spectacle, — between man and nature. Hence arises a pleasure mixed with awe; I may say, a low degree of the sublime is felt from the fact, probably, that man is hereby apprized, that, whilst the world is a spectacle, something in himself is stable.

2. In a higher manner, the poet communicates the same pleasure. By a few strokes he delineates, as on air, the sun, the mountain, the camp, the city, the hero, the maiden, not different from what we know them, but only lifted from the ground and afloat before the eye. He unfixes the land and the sea, makes them revolve around the axis of his primary thought, and dis-

poses them anew. Possessed himself by a heroic passion, he uses matter as symbols of it. The sensual man conforms thoughts to things; the poet conforms things to his thoughts. The one esteems nature as rooted and fast; the other, as fluid, and impresses his being thereon. To him, the refractory world is ductile and flexible; he invests dust and stones with humanity, and makes them the words of the Reason. The imagination may be defined to be, the use which the Reason makes of the material world. Shakspeare possesses the power of subordinating nature for the purposes of expression, beyond all poets. His imperial muse tosses the creation like a bauble from hand to hand, to embody any capricious shade of thought that is uppermost in his mind. The remotest spaces of nature are visited, and the farthest sundered things are brought together, by a subtile spiritual connexion. We are made aware that magnitude of material things is merely relative, and all objects shrink and expand to serve the passion of the poet. Thus, in his sonnets, the lays of birds, the scents and dyes of flowers, he finds to be the *shadow* of his beloved; time, which keeps her from him, is his *chest;* the suspicion she has awakened, is her *ornament;*

> The ornament of beauty is Suspect,
> A crow which flies in heaven's sweetest air.

His passion is not the fruit of chance; it swells, as he speaks, to a city, or a state.

> No, it was builded far from accident;
> It suffers not in smiling pomp, nor falls
> Under the brow of thralling discontent;
> It fears not policy, that heretic,
> That works on leases of short numbered hours,
> But all alone stands hugely politic.

In the strength of his constancy, the Pyramids seem to him recent and transitory. And the freshness of youth and love dazzles him with its resemblance to morning.

> Take those lips away
> Which so sweetly were forsworn;
> And those eyes, — the break of day,
> Lights that do mislead the morn.

The wild beauty of this hyperbole, I may say, in passing, it would not be easy to match in literature.

This transfiguration which all material objects undergo through the passion of the poet,—this power which he exerts, at any moment, to magnify the small, to micrify the great,—might be illustrated by a thousand examples from his Plays. I have before me the Tempest, and will cite only these few lines.

> ARIEL. The strong based promontory
> Have I made shake, and by the spurs plucked up
> The pine and cedar.

Prospero calls for music to sooth the frantic Alonzo, and his companions ;

> A solemn air, and the best comforter
> To an unsettled fancy, cure thy brains
> Now useless, boiled within thy skull.

Again ;

> The charm dissolves apace
> And, as the morning steals upon the night,
> Melting the darkness, so their rising senses
> Begin to chase the ignorant fumes that mantle
> Their clearer reason.

> Their understanding
> Begins to swell: and the approaching tide
> Will shortly fill the reasonable shores
> That now lie foul and muddy.

The perception of real affinities between events, (that is to say, of *ideal* affinities, for those only are real,) enables the poet thus to make free with the most imposing forms and phenomena of the world, and to assert the predominance of the soul.

3. Whilst thus the poet delights us by animating nature like a creator, with his own thoughts, he differs from the philosopher only herein, that the one proposes Beauty as his main end; the other Truth. But, the philosopher, not less than the poet, postpones the apparent order and relations of things to the empire of thought. "The problem of philosophy," according to Plato, "is, for all that exists conditionally, to find a ground unconditioned and absolute." It proceeds on the faith that a law determines all phenomena, which being known, the phenomena can be predicted. That law, when in the

mind, is an idea. Its beauty is infinite. The true philosopher and the true poet are one, and a beauty, which is truth, and a truth, which is beauty, is the aim of both. Is not the charm of one of Plato's or Aristotle's definitions, strictly like that of the Antigone of Sophocles? It is, in both cases, that a spiritual life has been imparted to nature; that the solid seeming block of matter has been pervaded and dissolved by a thought; that this feeble human being has penetrated the vast masses of nature with an informing soul, and recognised itself in their harmony, that is, seized their law. In physics, when this is attained, the memory disburthens itself of its cumbrous catalogues of particulars, and carries centuries of observation in a single formula.

Thus even in physics, the material is ever degraded before the spiritual. The astronomer, the geometer, rely on their irrefragable analysis, and disdain the results of observation. The sublime remark of Euler on his law of arches, "This will be found contrary to all experience, yet is true;" had already transferred nature into the mind, and left matter like an outcast corpse.

4. Intellectual science has been observed to beget invariably a doubt of the existence of matter. Turgot said, "He that has never doubted the existence of matter, may be assured he has no aptitude for metaphysical inquiries." It fastens the attention upon immortal necessary uncreated natures, that is, upon Ideas; and in their beautiful and majestic presence, we feel that our outward being is a dream and a shade. Whilst we wait in this Olympus of gods, we think of nature as an appendix to the soul. We ascend into their region, and know that these are the thoughts of the Supreme Being. "These are they who were set up from everlasting, from the beginning, or ever the earth was. When he prepared the heavens, they were there; when he established the clouds above, when he strengthened the fountains of the deep. Then they were by him, as one brought up with him. Of them took he counsel."

Their influence is proportionate. As objects of science, they are accessible to few men. Yet all men are capable of being raised by piety or by passion, into their region. And no man touches these divine natures, without becoming, in some degree, himself divine. Like a new soul, they renew the body. We become physically nimble and lightsome; we tread on air; life is no longer irksome, and we think it will never be so. No man fears age or misfortune or death, in their serene company, for he is transported out of the district of change. Whilst we behold unveiled the nature of Justice and Truth, we learn the difference between the absolute and the conditional or relative. We apprehend the absolute. As it were, for the first time, *we exist*. We become immortal, for we learn that time and space are relations of matter; that, with a perception of truth, or a virtuous will, they have no affinity.

5. Finally, religion and ethics, which may be fitly called, — the practice of ideas, or the introduction of ideas into life, — have an analo-

gous effect with all lower culture, in degrading nature and suggesting its dependence on spirit. Ethics and religion differ herein; that the one is the system of human duties commencing from man; the other, from God. Religion includes the personality of God; Ethics does not. They are one to our present design. They both put nature under foot. The first and last lesson of religion is, "The things that are seen, are temporal; the things that are unseen are eternal." It puts an affront upon nature. It does that for the unschooled, which philosophy does for Berkeley and Viasa. The uniform language that may be heard in the churches of the most ignorant sects, is, — 'Contemn the unsubstantial shows of the world; they are vanities, dreams, shadows, unrealities; seek the realities of religion.' The devotee flouts nature. Some theosophists have arrived at a certain hostility and indignation towards matter, as the Manichean and Plotinus. They distrusted in themselves any looking back to these flesh-pots of Egypt. Plotinus was ashamed of his body. In short, they might all better say of matter, what Michael Angelo said of external beauty, "it is the frail and weary weed, in which God dresses the soul, which he has called into time."

It appears that motion, poetry, physical and intellectual science, and religion, all tend to affect our convictions of the reality of the external world. But I own there is something ungrateful in expanding too curiously the particulars of the general proposition, that all culture tends to imbue us with idealism. I have no hostility to nature, but a child's love to it. I expand and live in the warm day like corn and melons. Let us speak her fair. I do not wish to fling stones at my beautiful mother, nor soil my gentle nest. I only wish to indicate the true position of nature in regard to man, wherein to establish man, all right education tends; as the ground which to attain is the object of human life, that is, of man's connexion with nature. Culture inverts the vulgar views of nature, and brings the mind to call that apparent, which it uses to call real, and that real, which it uses to call visionary. Children, it is true, believe in the external world. The belief that it appears only, is an afterthought, but with culture, this faith will as surely arise on the mind as did the first.

The advantage of the ideal theory over the popular faith, is this, that it presents the world in precisely that view which is most desirable to the mind. It is, in fact, the view which Reason, both speculative and practical, that is, philosophy and virtue, take. For, seen in the light of thought, the world always is phenomenal; and virtue subordinates it to the mind. Idealism sees the world in God. It beholds the whole circle of persons and things, of actions and events, of country and religion, not as painfully accumulated, atom after atom, act after act, in an aged creeping Past, but as one vast picture, which God paints on the instant eternity, for the contemplation of the soul. Therefore the soul holds itself off from a too trivial and microscopic study of the universal tablet. It respects the end too much, to immerse itself in the means. It sees something more important in Christianity, than the scandals of ecclesiastical history or the niceties of criticism; and, very incurious concerning persons or miracles, and not at all disturbed by chasms of historical evidence, it accepts from God the phenomenon, as it finds it, as the pure and awful form of religion in the world. It is not hot and passionate at the appearance of what it calls its own good or bad fortune, at the union or opposition of other persons. No man is its enemy. It accepts whatsoever befals, as part of its lesson. It is a watcher more than a doer, and it is a doer, only that it may the better watch.

CHAPTER VII.

SPIRIT.

It is essential to a true theory of nature and of man, that it should contain somewhat progressive. Uses that are exhausted or that may be, and facts that end in the statement, cannot be all that is true of this brave lodging wherein man is harbored, and wherein all his faculties find appropriate and endless exercise. And all the uses of nature admit of being summed in one, which yields the activity of man an infinite scope. Through all its kingdoms, to the suburbs and outskirts of things, it is faithful to the cause whence it had its origin. It always speaks of Spirit. It suggests the absolute. It is a perpetual effect. It is a great shadow pointing always to the sun behind us.

The aspect of nature is devout. Like the figure of Jesus, she stands with bended head, and hands folded upon the breast. The happiest man is he who learns from nature the lesson of worship.

Of that ineffable essence which we call Spirit, he that thinks most, will say least. We can foresee God in the coarse and, as it were, distant phenomena of matter; but when we try to define and describe himself, both language and thought desert us, and we are as helpless as fools and savages. That essence refuses to be recorded in propositions, but when man has worshipped him intellectually, the noblest ministry of nature is to stand as the apparition of God. It is the great organ through which the universal spirit speaks to the individual, and strives to lead back the individual to it.

When we consider Spirit, we see that the views already presented do not include the whole circumference of man. We must add some related thoughts.

Three problems are put by nature to the mind; What is matter? Whence is it? and Whereto? The first of these questions only, the ideal theory answers. Idealism saith: matter is a phenomenon, not a substance. Idealism acquaints us with the total disparity between the evidence of our own being, and the evidence of the world's being. The one is perfect; the other, incapable of any assurance; the mind is a part of the nature of things; the world is a divine dream, from which we may presently awake to the glories and certainties of day. Idealism is a hypothesis to account for nature by other principles than those of carpentry and chemistry. Yet, if it only deny the existence of matter, it does not satisfy the demands of the spirit. It leaves God out of me. It leaves me in the splendid labyrinth of my perceptions, to wander without end. Then the heart resists it, because it baulks the affections in denying substantive being to men and women. Nature is so pervaded with human life, that there is something of humanity in all, and in every particular. But this theory makes nature foreign to me, and does not account for that consanguinity which we acknowledge to it.

Problem of idealism

Let it stand then, in the present state of our knowledge, merely as a useful introductory hypothesis, serving to apprize us of the eternal distinction between the soul and the world.

But when, following the invisible steps of thought, we come to inquire, Whence is matter? and Whereto? many truths arise to us out of the recesses of consciousness. We learn that the highest is present to the soul of man, that the dread universal essence, which is not wisdom, or love, or beauty, or power, but all in one, and each entirely, is that for which all things exist, and that by which they are; that spirit creates; that behind nature, throughout nature, spirit is present; that spirit is one and not compound; that spirit does not act upon us from without, that is, in space and time, but spiritually, or through ourselves. Therefore, that spirit, that is, the Supreme Being, does not build up nature around us, but puts it forth through us, as the life of the tree puts forth new branches and leaves through the pores of the old. As a plant upon the earth, so a man rests upon the bosom of God; he is nourished by unfailing fountains, and draws, at his need, inexhaustible power. Who can set bounds to the possibilities of man? Once inspire the infinite, by being admitted to behold the absolute natures of justice and truth, and we learn that man has access to the entire mind of the Creator, is himself the creator in the finite. This view, which admonishes me where the sources of wisdom and power lie, and points to virtue as to

> "The golden key
> Which opes the palace of eternity,"

carries upon its face the highest certificate of truth, because it animates me to create my own world through the purification of my soul.

The world proceeds from the same spirit as the body of man. It is a remoter and inferior incarnation of God, a projection of God in the unconscious. But it differs from the body in one important respect. It is not, like that, now subjected to the human will. Its serene order is inviolable by us. It is therefore, to us, the present expositor of the divine mind. It is a fixed point whereby we may measure our departure. As we degenerate, the contrast between us and our house is more evident. We are as much strangers in nature, as we are aliens from God. We do not understand the notes of birds. The fox and the deer run away from us; the bear and tiger rend us. We do not know the uses of more than a few plants, as corn and the apple, the potato and the vine. Is not the landscape, every glimpse of which hath a grandeur, a face of him? Yet this may show us what discord is between man and nature, for you cannot freely admire a noble landscape, if laborers are digging in the field hard by. The poet finds something ridiculous in his delight, until he is out of the sight of men.

CHAPTER VIII.

PROSPECTS.

In inquiries respecting the laws of the world and the frame of things, the highest reason is always the truest. That which seems faintly possible — it is so refined, is often faint and dim because it is deepest seated in the mind among the eternal verities. Empirical science is apt to cloud the sight, and, by the very knowledge of functions and processes, to bereave the student of the manly contemplation of the whole. The savant becomes unpoetic. But the best read naturalist who lends an entire and devout attention to truth, will see that there remains much to learn of his relation to the world, and that it is not to be learned by any addition or subtraction or other comparison of known quantities, but is arrived at by untaught sallies of the spirit, by a continual self-recovery, and by entire humility. He will perceive that there are far more excellent qualities in the student than preciseness and infallibility; that a guess is often more fruitful than an indisputable affirmation, and that a dream may let us deeper into the secret of nature than a hundred concerted experiments.

For, the problems to be solved are precisely those which the physiologist and the naturalist omit to state. It is not so pertinent to man to know all the individuals of the animal kingdom, as it is to know whence and whereto is this tyrannizing unity in his constitution, which evermore separates and classifies things, endeavouring to reduce the most diverse to one form. When I behold a rich landscape, it is less to my purpose to recite correctly the order and superposition of the strata, than to know why all thought of multitude is lost in a tranquil sense of unity. I cannot greatly honor minuteness in details, so long as there is no hint to explain the relation between things and thoughts; no ray upon the *metaphysics* of conchology, of botany, of the arts, to show the relation of the forms of flowers, shells, animals, architecture, to the mind, and build science upon ideas. In a cabinet of natural history, we become sensible of a certain occult recognition and sympathy in regard to the most bizarre forms of beast, fish, and insect. The American who has been confined, in his own country, to the sight of buildings designed after foreign models, is surprised on entering York Minster or St. Peter's at Rome, by the feeling that these structures are imitations also, — faint copies of an invisible archetype. Nor has science sufficient humanity, so long as the naturalist overlooks that wonderful congruity which subsists between man and the world; of which he is lord, not because he is the most subtile inhabitant, but because he is its head and heart, and finds something of himself in every great and small thing, in every mountain stratum, in every new law of color, fact of astronomy, or atmospheric influence which observation or analysis lay open. A perception of this mystery inspires the muse of George Herbert, the beautiful psalmist of the seventeenth century. The following lines are part of his little poem on Man.

"Man is all symmetry,
Full of proportions, one limb to another,
And to all the world besides.
Each part may call the farthest, brother;
For head with foot hath private amity,
And both with moons and tides.

"Nothing hath got so far
But man hath caught and kept it as his prey;
His eyes dismount the highest star;
He is in little all the sphere.
Herbs gladly cure our flesh, because that they
Find their acquaintance there.

"For us, the winds do blow,
The earth doth rest, heaven move, and fountains flow;
Nothing we see, but means our good,
As our delight, or as our treasure;
The whole is either our cupboard of food,
Or cabinet of pleasure.

"The stars have us to bed:
Night draws the curtain; which the sun withdraws.
Music and light attend our head.

All things unto our flesh are kind,
In their descent and being; to our mind,
In their ascent and cause.

"More servants wait on man
Than he 'll take notice of. In every path,
He treads down that which doth befriend him
When sickness makes him pale and wan.
Oh mighty love! Man is one world, and hath
Another to attend him."

The perception of this class of truths makes the eternal attraction which draws men to science, but the end is lost sight of in attention to the means. In view of this half-sight of science, we accept the sentence of Plato, that, "poetry comes nearer to vital truth than history." Every surmise and vaticination of the mind is entitled to a certain respect, and we learn to prefer imperfect theories, and sentences, which contain glimpses of truth, to digested systems which have no one valuable suggestion. A wise writer will feel that the ends of study and composition are best answered by announcing undiscovered regions of thought, and so communicating, through hope, new activity to the torpid spirit.

I shall therefore conclude this essay with some traditions of man and nature, which a certain poet sang to me; and which, as they have always been in the world, and perhaps reappear to every bard, may be both history and prophecy.

The foundations of man are not in matter, but in spirit. But the element of spirit is eternity. To it, therefore, the longest series of events, the oldest chronologies are young and recent. In the cycle of the universal man, from whom the known individuals proceed, centuries are points, and all history is but the epoch of one degradation.

'We distrust and deny inwardly our sympathy with nature. We own and disown our relation to it, by turns. We are, like Nebuchadnezzar, dethroned, bereft of reason, and eating grass like an ox. But who can set limits to the remedial force of spirit?

'A man is a god in ruins. When men are innocent, life shall be longer, and shall pass into the immortal, as gently as we awake from dreams. Now, the world would be insane and rabid, if these disorganizations should last for hundreds of years. It is kept in check by death and infancy. Infancy is the perpetual Messiah, which comes into the arms of fallen men, and pleads with them to return to paradise.

'Man is the dwarf of himself. Once he was permeated and dissolved by spirit. He filled nature with his overflowing currents. Out from him sprang the sun and moon; from man, the sun; from woman, the moon. The laws of his mind, the periods of his actions externized themselves into day and night, into the year and the seasons. But, having made for himself this huge shell, his waters retired; he no longer fills the veins and veinlets; he is shrunk to a drop. He sees, that the structure still fits him, but fits him colossally. Say, rather, once it fitted him, now it corresponds to him from far and on high.

He adores timidly his own work. Now is man the follower of the sun, and woman the follower of the moon. Yet sometimes he starts in his slumber, and wonders at himself and his house, and muses strangely at the resemblance betwixt him and it. He perceives that if his law is still paramount, if still he have elemental power, "if his word is sterling yet in nature," it is not conscious power, it is not inferior but superior to his will. It is Instinct.' Thus my Orphic poet sang.

At present, man applies to nature but half his force. He works on the world with his understanding alone. He lives in it, and masters it by a penny-wisdom ; and he that works most in it, is but a half-man, and whilst his arms are strong and his digestion good, his mind is imbruted and he is a selfish savage. His relation to nature, his power over it, is through the understanding ; as by manure ; the economic use of fire, wind, water, and the mariner's needle ; steam, coal, chemical agriculture ; the repairs of the human body by the dentist and the surgeon. This is such a resumption of power, as if a banished king should buy his territories inch by inch, instead of vaulting at once into his throne. Meantime, in the thick darkness, there are not wanting gleams of a better light, — occasional examples of the action of man upon nature with his entire force, — with reason as well as understanding. Such examples are; the traditions of miracles in the earliest antiquity of all nations; the history of Jesus Christ; the achievements of a principle, as in religious and political revolutions, and in the abolition of the Slave-trade; the miracles of enthusiasm, as those reported of Swedenborg, Hohenlohe, and the Shakers; many obscure and yet contested facts, now arranged under the name of Animal Magnetism; prayer; eloquence; self-healing; and the wisdom of children. These are examples of Reason's momentary grasp of the sceptre; the exertions of a power which exists not in time or space, but an instantaneous in-streaming causing power. The difference between the actual and the ideal force of man is happily figured by the schoolmen, in saying, that the knowledge of man is an evening knowledge, *vespertina cognitio*, but that of God is a morning knowledge, *matutina cognitio*.

The problem of restoring to the world original and eternal beauty, is solved by the redemption of the soul. The ruin or the blank, that we see when we look at nature, is in our own eye. The axis of vision is not coincident with the axis of things, and so they appear not transparent but opake. The reason why the world lacks unity, and lies broken and in heaps, is, because man is disunited with himself. He cannot be a naturalist, until he satisfies all the demands of the spirit. Love is as much its demand, as perception. Indeed, neither can be perfect without the other. In the uttermost meaning of the words, thought is devout, and devotion is thought. Deep calls unto deep. But in actual life, the marriage is not celebrated. There are innocent men who worship God after the tradition of their fathers, but their sense of duty has not yet extended to the use of all their

faculties. And there are patient naturalists, but they freeze their subject under the wintry light of the understanding. Is not prayer also a study of truth, — a sally of the soul into the unfound infinite? No man ever prayed heartily, without learning something. But when a faithful thinker, resolute to detach every object from personal relations, and see it in the light of thought, shall, at the same time, kindle science with the fire of the holiest affections, then will God go forth anew into the creation.

It will not need, when the mind is prepared for study, to search for objects. The invariable mark of wisdom is to see the miraculous in the common. What is a day? What is a year? What is summer? What is woman? What is a child? What is sleep? To our blindness, these things seem unaffecting. We make fables to hide the baldness of the fact and conform it, as we say, to the higher law of the mind. But when the fact is seen under the light of an idea, the gaudy fable fades and shrivels. We behold the real higher law. To the wise, therefore, a fact is true poetry, and the most beautiful of fables. These wonders are brought to our own door. You also are a man. Man and woman, and their social life, poverty, labor, sleep, fear, fortune, are known to you. Learn that none of these things is superficial, but that each phenomenon hath its roots in the faculties and affections of the mind. Whilst the abstract question occupies your intellect, nature brings it in the concrete to be solved by your hands. It were a wise inquiry for the closet, to compare, point by point, especially at remarkable crises in life, our daily history, with the rise and progress of ideas in the mind.

So shall we come to look at the world with new eyes. It shall answer the endless inquiry of the intellect, — What is truth? and of the affections, — What is good? by yielding itself passive to the educated Will. Then shall come to pass what my poet said; 'Nature is not fixed but fluid. Spirit alters, moulds, makes it. The immobility or bruteness of nature, is the absence of spirit; to pure spirit, it is fluid, it is volatile, it is obedient. Every spirit builds itself a house; and beyond its house, a world; and beyond its world, a heaven. Know then, that the world exists for you. For you is the phenomenon perfect. What we are, that only can we see. All that Adam had, all that Cæsar could, you have and can do. Adam called his house, heaven and earth; Cæsar called his house, Rome; you perhaps call yours, a cobler's trade; a hundred acres of ploughed land; or a scholar's garret. Yet line for line and point for point, your dominion is as great as theirs, though without fine names. Build, therefore, your own world. As fast as you conform your life to the pure idea in your mind, that will unfold its great proportions. A correspondent revolution in things will attend the influx of the spirit. So fast will disagreeable appearances, swine, spiders, snakes, pests, mad-houses, prisons, enemies, vanish; they are temporary and shall be no more seen. The sordor and filths of nature, the sun shall dry up, and the wind exhale. As when the summer comes from the south, the snow-banks melt, and the face of the earth becomes green before it, so shall the advancing spirit create its ornaments along its path, and carry with it the beauty it visits, and the song which enchants it; it shall draw beautiful faces, and warm hearts, and wise discourse, and heroic acts, around its way, until evil is no more seen. The kingdom of man over nature, which cometh not with observation, — a dominion such as now is beyond his dream of God, — he shall enter without more wonder than the blind man feels who is gradually restored to perfect sight.'